If I
You Can

If you can dream it, you can do it!

Reading this book will be one of the best decisions
you will ever make.

Sally Eichhorst

...inspire the world
with words.

Reach Publishers
Self-publishers and Distributors of all books

By Sally Eichhorst
Get Your Act Together

By Warren Veenman & Sally Eichhorst
Unleash Your Full Potential
Dare To Succeed
A Pocket Full of Inspiration
A Little Burst of Inspiration
Where Has My Ceiling Gone?

ISBN 0 620 27943 5

Published by Reach Publishers, P.O.Box, 1384, Wandsbeck, South Africa, 3631
Printed and bound by Pinetown Printers (Pty) Ltd, 16 Ivy Road, Pinetown, 3600
Edited by Janine Williams
Cover designed by Reach Publishers

Website: **www.aimtoinspire.com**

E-mail: **reach @webstorm.co.za**

This book is dedicated to the memory of
Dale Rene' Berman

A pure and gentle soul is at last flying free.
She fought for many years against the dying of the light.
At last she is at peace and her light will shine forever
within all the lives she touched.
I love you Mom.

Contents

A Chapter of Life

Life is like a book with many different chapters.
Some tell of tragedy, others of triumph.
Some chapters are dull and ordinary,
others intense and exciting.

The key to being a success in life
is to never stop on a difficult page,
to never quit on a tough chapter.

Champions have the courage to keep turning the pages
because they know a better chapter lies ahead.

Author unknown

The Journey Begins...

*A rose only becomes beautiful and blesses others
when it opens up and blooms.
Its greatest tragedy is to stay in a tight-closed bud,
never fulfilling its potential.*

Anon

I've done it! I've made a remarkable discovery that has unearthed a secret. I came upon this find along my journey through life and now I want you to come with me as I uncover the mystery in the following pages. Step by step, I'll be with you, as we piece the puzzle together and in the end you will share the secret with me, as it unfolds and your life will be better off for it.

I invite you to join me on an adventurous journey of achievement and fulfillment as I show you how to enjoy your trip through life, no matter what has and will still happen to you along the way. That is what this book is all about. It aims to show you how to make the most of your life by living it to the fullest and achieving your dreams.

Life is a play. It's not its length, but its performance that counts.

Seneca

This book shares a number of remarkable and moving stories and powerful insights that will help you to make your journey through life a little less difficult and a lot more meaningful.

Read everything carefully and really think about what you are reading so that you can apply it to your life. I urge you to actively take part in all the practical exercises and explore the various topics and concepts, letting everything sink in and make a lasting impression on you. Only then will you benefit fully from this book.

It is the type of book that you should read again and again to keep you inspired and motivated to live your life to the full. The fact is that not many people can remain self-motivated every single day of their lives. We all need a gentle boost and reminder every now and again, that life is short and should be made sweet, not bitter. This book aims to make your life a whole lot sweeter. Our journey has begun...

Chapter 1

If I Can, You Can!

If you feel that your life is empty, why not try putting more into it?
Sally Eichhorst

No one in and of themselves is extraordinary. We are all ordinary people. Even the greatest achievers of our time were but ordinary people and the most successful people today are all ordinary people. What makes them extraordinary is what they do with their lives - ordinary people doing extraordinary things.

You and I are both ordinary people but we too can create an extraordinary life by living out our dreams and striving always to live life to the fullest.

We are all born with remarkable potential, into a world with limitless opportunities. No matter who we are and what our circumstances, there comes a time when we can choose how we will live. We can choose to waste our potential and miss out on all the opportunities available to us or we can choose to make the most of our potential and seek out all available opportunities.

I've seen poor people grow rich. I've seen disabled people succeed. I've seen uneducated people rise to the top. I've met those who should have been miserable and unhappy due to their circumstances, rise above their situations to live happy and fulfilled lives. These are all ordinary people, perhaps even less fortunate than you and I who have chosen to make the most of their lives despite their circumstances. If they can, why not you?

I am living the life of my dreams. I refuse to be a spectator watching life pass me by. I have carefully built the existence I want and am extremely happy in it. Anyone can do it. **If I can, you can! This book is about how you can do it.**

ANYONE CAN ACHIEVE THEIR DREAMS

> *Every great achievement was once impossible.*
>
> **Anon**

Don't let anyone fool you. Achieving your goals and making your dreams a reality is hard work. For most of us there are no shortcuts to easy street. If you want something badly enough, you have to work for it. However, this makes the rewards all the more sweet, like coming across a waterfall of fresh cascading water after a two day hike in the blistering hot desert. Without worthy goals to strive for there would be no sense of achievement and joy in our accomplishments. Goals often test our limits, pushing us harder than ever before. Many of us never fully realize the potential strength and power within us until we attempt to drive ourselves towards a goal, refusing to give up and eventually beating the odds and accomplishing what was once only a distant dream.

If you can dream it, you can do it! It's just a matter of work. Are you up to it? As I said earlier, anyone can make their dreams a reality. By mastering the following 6 - part work theory you can make your journey through life an adventurous one. It is sure to be exciting and inspiring reading, full of remarkable stories and powerful insights as well as plenty of advice and practical input.

If you want to make the most of your journey through life by achieving your dreams, then read on.

> *Don't dismiss your dreams. To be without dreams is to be without hope; to be without hope is to be without purpose.*
>
> **Nancye Sims**

THE 6 - PART WORK THEORY

Part 1. Mind Work
Part 2. Character Work
Part 3. Dream Work
Part 4. Ground Work
Part 5. Dredge Work
Part 6. Maintenance Work

Hard work without talent is a shame,
but talent without hard work is a tragedy.

Robert Half

Come with me through the following chapters as I take you through each part step by step. Think about what you are reading. Let it filter through and make an impression on you.

Part 1

Mind Work

A Love of Life

It's in my blood; I flow with it.
It's in my lungs; I breathe it.
It's in my heart; I feel it.
It fills every cell; I thrive on it.
It's all around me; I see it, hear it, love it and I truly need it.
It fills the world with wonder and touches everything.
I'll fight for it, cherish it, share it and treat it like a King.
IT is LIFE!
A love of Life has made me content to the core.
This love of Life has brought good things to my door.
There are those who choose to run from Life, hide from it or waste it.
I choose to embrace Life, love it and make the most of it.
In return, my world is one of peace, happiness and contentment.
Age has rewarded me with smile lines, not frown lines
and a Life more precious than all the world's gold mines.
My taste of Life is so delicious, that I am always hungry for more.
More to see, more to do, more to feel!
There is always more to Life if you have
A Love of Life!

Sally Eichhorst

Chapter 2

Spring-Cleaning Your Mind!

Life is full of surprises.
Some leave a bitter taste in your mouth,
while others leave the sweet sensation of chocolate.
The trick is to never allow any bad taste to linger,
but rather to dull it with the memory of your last sweet sensation.
Sally Eichhorst

A man in his journey through Life looked old before his time. Weak and exhausted, he dragged his feet in a slow shuffle. His back was bent with the burden of his baggage and his face was set in a deep frown. His eyes betrayed his life's story - pain, disappointment and resentment.

'Why don't you rest awhile,' said the 'Spring-cleaner'. 'You look tired and overburdened. What is it you're dragging along with you everywhere in that enormous bag? It looks so heavy and uncomfortable to carry and I can see it's causing you pain.'

The man shuffled to a standstill with a deep sigh and his legs wobbled unsteadily under the strain of the enormous burden still balanced upon his shoulders. 'I've had this bag as far back as I can recall' he said. 'I've carried it with me through Life and everyday it seems to get heavier, weighing me down like a ball and chain, yet I can't get rid of it. It's like it's part of me and we're shackled together by some invisible bond. I know it's held me back in Life and there are days like today when I feel I just can't go on. The burden I carry has become unbearable and I almost wish my journey through Life was at an end.'

The 'Spring-cleaner' took pity on the man as he had done on so many before him. 'They call me 'The Spring-cleaner' he said. 'I'd like to help you if you let me?'

The man's eyes shone with hope and he eagerly nodded his approval. 'Anything, I'll do anything to lessen the load' he said.

'Do you know what spring-cleaning is?' he asked.

'Sure, it means cleaning out your closet or your home by getting rid of all the old things,' said the man.

'That's right,' agreed the 'Spring-cleaner'. 'Now, have you ever spring-cleaned your mind?' he asked.

'What do you mean? I have no idea what you're getting at!' said the man with exasperation.

'Well, just as you regularly spring-clean your home or closet, you should regularly spring-clean your mind. In other words, take the time to review your life, all the 'old baggage' - the hurts, the jealousies, the resentments, the painful memories, the failures - all the bad old stuff you've hoarded throughout the years. Do some serious spring-cleaning and get rid of it all. You certainly don't need it! You see, this bag you've been carrying for most of your life is filled with all your 'old baggage' and you keep adding to it as you progress through Life. The invisible bond that shackles you to the bag is your own doing. Only you can undo it. You need to learn to let go. Spring-clean your mind and throw the 'trash' away. Let go of all the old hurts, bad memories and resentments and only then will you be able to move forward freely, unburdened by a bag full of pain, anger and regrets.'

The Spring-cleaner and the man talked for many hours. Hours turned to days and days to weeks until one day the man was ready to leave. It was not the same man who had arrived weak, exhausted and prematurely aged weeks before. This was a changed man - younger in mind and body, stronger physically and mentally, relaxed and energized. His bag was empty, as though his journey had only just begun and he leapt joyously into the future like a child embarking upon a new adventure!

Don't carry grudges, for they are the heaviest of all life's burdens.

Author unknown

Now I want you, yes you the reader to do some spring-cleaning. All I want you to do is to take pen and paper and find a quiet place where you can be alone for awhile. Now write down all the negative things you have carried with you through life. You see Life is like a big hold-all-bag. You throw all your memories, experiences, hurts, resentments etc. in this bag and soon you're dragging a huge, heavy, overloaded amount of unnecessary baggage.

I want you to write it all down and get it out of your system, like a cleansing process. Just writing it all down has an amazing effect. It's like taking a weight off your shoulders and you'll feel like its time to start afresh with a new attitude and approach to life. Remarkably, many people have told me that it restored their spirit, awakening the person they once were before they accumulated all the old baggage.

For many years a friend of mine felt a great deal of resentment towards her mother for not being there when she needed her and for her weakness when she was around. She then decided to write a letter to her mother telling her exactly how she felt. She ended up writing 30 pages filled with all the hurtful things she'd kept bottled up for years. The most amazing thing was that once she had finished, she felt no need to send it. Just writing it all down had cleansed her somehow and put it out in the open as though it were now dealt with and over. She felt as though it was now time to move on and start anew. The mere act of writing it all down improved relations tremendously with her mother as she no longer felt all the pent-up emotions and resentment of the past. She had done some serious spring-cleaning and it had worked wonders!

You really need to do this. You'll be amazed at the effect! Perhaps you're still hurt and angry about a past relationship. Maybe your previous boss treated you badly. You could still be feeling angry and vengeful toward someone who let you down or hurt you. You could have had one or more bad experiences, which still haunt you.

Whatever old baggage you carry, you must realize that the past is gone and to progress and bring out the best in yourself, you have to start shutting out all the old hurts, disappointments and bad experiences from your mind. Come on, make a fresh start now, by getting rid of all your old baggage and cleansing your mind.

Letting go is not a matter of forgetting, denying or giving up,
but rather accepting and moving on.

Sally Eichhorst

SPRING-CLEANING AND TREES???

I adore trees. To me, they are a symbol of life, beauty, strength and nature. My garden is filled with trees of all shapes and sizes and I watch fondly as they grow, shed leaves, bear fruit and sustain life, year after year. Believe it or not, we can all learn a very important lesson about spring-cleaning from trees.

Let's imagine that a healthy, living tree ignorantly and greedily decides to hold on to this year's leaves even after they have served their purpose. What would happen? Slow but certain decay would result and eventually death. There would be no full and beautiful life to awaken in the spring, as there would be no room for the new leaves.

You see, as long as the tree is living and active, it is vital for it's survival to rid itself of the old leaves so that there may be room for the new. The only time a tree should ever cling to the old leaves is if it is dead already.

Like trees, we too must continually get rid of the old to make room for new and better things in life. Too many people cling desperately to old memories, hurts and beliefs instead of using them, learning from them and then letting go of them once they have served their purpose. Hoarding inevitably leads to some form of loss. Renewed gain comes only from using wisely, learning from and then letting go to welcome the new.

Don't try to relive yesterday for good or ill,
as it is forever gone.
Rather concentrate on what is happening
in your life today and be happy now!

Author unknown

Chapter 3

Believe You Can!

Belief is a powerful mechanism,
which can either drive you forward on the road to success
or drag you backwards along the road to failure.

Sally Eichhorst

THE TEMP TEACHER

'Danny, don't be silly! Surely you can see that the answer is clearly 2,' said Mrs. Brown with exasperation. 'Why you still cannot grasp such a simple exercise I'll never know! Goodness knows I've tried my best with you,' exclaimed Mrs. Brown as she looked sternly over her metal-rimmed glasses and fixed the young boy with a painfully penetrating gaze.

Danny lowered his eyes guiltily and blushed profusely as he felt all the eyes in the classroom singling him out. He could hear some of them laughing at him, making fun of his 'stupidity.

'Why am I so stupid?' thought Danny. 'Why can't I just be like everyone else? What's wrong with me? I wish I could just be normal. Mom and Dad are probably so disappointed in me. I'll bet they don't really love me. They just make believe and wish I were someone else.

The lunch bell interrupted his thoughts and all the kids rushed past him in a noisy, bustling jostle for the door. Danny made for an empty bench on the playground and quietly ate his lunch in solitude. Kids laughed, ran and wrestled one another playfully all around him, but Danny was too preoccupied with his own worrying thoughts to even notice them.

'I'm so stupid! No one wants to be with someone who's so stupid. I can't do anything right. I'm just stupid, stupid, stupid!' he repeated angrily to himself.

Danny battled through his first year of school, keeping his silly ideas to himself, never daring to speak out and confirm what his teacher, classmates and now he too knew to be true - he was stupid!

What once was a bright, confident and cheerful child became a withdrawn loner, lacking in self-confidence and fighting a mountain of insecurities. He became disinterested in learning as he felt he was stupid anyway, so what was the point of even trying.

It was the second term of Grade 2 and there was great excitement in the classroom. Danny sat quietly in the corner wondering what the nervous buzz was about. The Principal walked in followed closely by a lady Danny had never seen before. She was very short and thin, with pointy ears and a small pointy nose. She had big blue eyes that seemed to light up when she saw the children and a great big mouth that stretched ever so wide and formed the biggest smile Danny had ever seen.

'This is Miss Bentley. She will be stepping in as a temp. Teacher for the next 6 months as Mrs. Brown is away indefinitely on sick leave,' said the Principal before turning and marching out again, leaving the Pixie-like Miss Bentley behind.

'To this day I believe that Miss Bentley was a magic Pixie sent to rescue the lost and confused child I'd become,' recalled a much older and happier Danny.

Miss Bentley was secretly enchanted by the little boy in the corner, with the big, sad brown eyes, much like a guilty puppy giving you its most sorrowful look to encourage forgiveness. At an age when most children were brimming with self-confidence and full of the joys of life, this little guy looked like he carried the world on his shoulders. He never raised a hand to question or answer anything, never spoke unless directed to and never looked you in the eyes, instead always guiltily averting his gaze. Yet she sensed a depth to him. There was a sparkle of intelligence in those dark eyes that the boy almost hid with fierce determination. Why? Miss Bentley made it her secret mission to find out what was wrong with Danny, if anything?

'Danny, let's say Mary has four apples and Jane has none. If Mary decides to share her apples with Jane, how many apples will Jane get?' asked Miss Bentley.

Danny squirmed uncomfortably in his seat wishing he could melt away into it and escape the question. There was a deafening silence as everyone waited expectantly for his answer. 'I'm not sure,' he stammered. Before Miss Bentley could go on, one of Danny's classmates yelled out 'It's 2 apples, you Dummy!' This was followed by a roar of laughter from the rest of the class.

Danny fought back his tears and wished he could make it all go away - the teasing, the laughing, the embarrassment and mostly the hurt!

Just then the bell rang noisily to end the school day and Danny was relieved at the thought of escape. However Miss Bentley stopped him at the door and asked him to stay behind, as she wanted to talk to him. He knew what was coming. She wanted to scold him for being so stupid. She probably wanted to warn him that she would tell his parents how stupid he was if he didn't start pulling up his socks.

Miss Bentley started rummaging around in her oversized bag and eventually found what she was looking for. To Danny's amazement she triumphantly clutched a box of Smarties. 'I love these things,' she said. 'I only share them with special little people like you. Want one?' she offered as she smiled down at the worried little face before her.

Danny was taken totally off guard and eyed the box of Smarties suspiciously.

'Come on, grab a few before I munch them all up,' she insisted.

'No thank you Miss Bentley,' said Danny politely.

'Why not? Don't you like Smarties?' asked Miss Bentley sincerely.

'I'm not special, so you shouldn't share them with me.' Danny answered, looking down at his shoes and once again blushing uncontrollably.

Miss Bentley was stunned. She wanted to hug him close and tell him over and over again just how special he is.

'Everyone is special in their own way Danny. We all have something special to offer that no one else has,' said Miss Bentley soothingly.

'Uh-uh. Not me. I'm just plain stupid! There's nothing special about that!' said Danny determinedly.

'Who says you're stupid?' asked Mrs. Bentley encouragingly.

'Everyone! Mrs. Brown says she can't understand why I can't answer questions like everyone else and why I always have to be silly and difficult. They all laugh at me because I'm never sure of the right answer. I guess they're right. It's just that I'm stupid. The other day Steve Thomas called me 'an idiot'. I suppose that means the same as stupid. So you see, I am stupid.' Danny finished off whilst biting his bottom lip nervously.

Miss Bentley had to fight to control her rising anger at Mrs. Brown and the cruelty of children in general. It broke her heart to listen to this little boy putting himself down so harshly and relentlessly. Because he was led to believe that he was stupid the poor little guy felt that he didn't even deserve a single Smartie.

'You know, that's kind of strange because I happen to think you're smart and I'm never wrong. In fact, I only share my Smarties with smart people. That's why they call them Smarties. Do you really think I would offer you any if I thought you weren't smart and special enough?' she asked with a warm reassuring smile.

'Well,' he said uncertainly with a thoughtful frown creasing his forehead whilst he studied the Pixie-like Miss Bentley and the Smarties with renewed interest.

Miss Bentley recognized the gleam of interest and once more noticed the spark of intelligence burning deep within the big brown eyes before her. How could anyone miss it? This boy has potential! So what's missing? What's the problem? Why can't he come up with the right answers? Why is he so disinterested in learning?

Her thoughts were interrupted by a small hand reaching out hesitantly towards the box of Smarties she still held out. A breakthrough!

The Smarties were good and Miss Bentley made him feel special. She thought he was smart and she made him feel like the most important person in the world.

She watched him slowly relax and it was amazing to see the worried frown she'd witnessed so often turn into a shy smile that brightened his face and lit up those big intelligent eyes like Christmas lights.

'Do you like learning Danny?' she ventured.

'I used to. But I'm not good at it, so now I don't really care for it much,' he replied through a mouth jam packed with Smarties.

'Why do you think you're not good at it?' she asked.

'Because I always have silly answers or I'm not exactly sure of the right answer,' he answered firmly.

'Do you remember the question I asked you earlier on today in class? You said you weren't sure of the answer. I didn't get a chance to ask you why you weren't sure or what you thought the answer was. Do you remember?' asked Miss Bentley encouragingly.

Danny wished Miss Bentley hadn't asked the question again. He knew what she wanted him to answer, but he just wasn't sure that it was the right answer. She would just think that he was being silly and then she'd also call him stupid and wish she hadn't shared her Smarties with him. He liked her so much and he really didn't want to disappoint her, but he just couldn't help the way he thought. He knew it wasn't normal and probably stupid, but he just didn't understand why he wasn't always sure of the right answer. To him, there often seemed to be more than one answer.

'Danny, remember the question - let's say Mary has 4 apples and Jane has none. If Mary decides to share her apples with Jane, how many apples will Jane get?' asked Miss Bentley and smiled patiently.

'I know you want me to answer 2, but I'm still not sure it's the right answer,' Danny said nervously, again avoiding Miss Bentley's eyes in case he saw mocking laughter or anger in them at his response.

'Look at me Danny,' she said and as he looked up into her large blue eyes he saw no anger, disappointment or mocking laughter. He saw warmth, caring and understanding. Is it possible that she could understand his silly ideas and answers? He knew instinctively that she would.

'Miss Bentley, you said Mary has 4 apples and Jane has none. Then you said, **if** Mary decides to share her apples with Jane, how many apples will Jane get? Well you see it's the **'if'** that's the problem. **'If'** means that she doesn't definitely decide to share her apples so how do I know for sure? Did she or didn't she decide to share her apples? And if she did decide to share them, you didn't say whether she shared all her apples equally with Jane. You see, sharing could mean only giving her a bite of each apple or only giving her one apple or maybe even three. I'm just not sure what the right answer is because there seems to be more than one answer depending on what really happened. ' Danny finished off and was immediately sorry for trying to explain himself as he mistook the look on Miss Bentley's face for horror.

In fact, Miss Bentley was staring wide-mouthed at him with absolute shock and awe. This boy was a genius! His thought processes and reasoning abilities were way above normal. Of course he was a total misfit amongst his classmates. How could they possibly understand him for he was way ahead of them. He was on a different intellectual level altogether - **a child genius!**

To Danny's relief Miss Bentley's face slowly transformed and her great big smile appeared, spreading from ear to ear and all at once she was suddenly hugging him tight and his little heart swelled with love and pride as she repeated again and again how smart and special he was.

Danny was indeed found to be a child genius. His I.Q. was well above average and stunned the educational authorities. Danny was moved into a school for gifted children where his intellect could be stimulated and allowed to grow.

The little boy who once believed he was stupid because he was led to believe this by teachers and peers was in fact a shining light of intelligence in a dull room of ignorance. If it were not for that one person in his life who believed in him and urged him to believe in himself and his abilities, his true genius may never have been discovered.

'Thank you Miss Bentley, "my magic pixie", for rescuing just another little lost soul.' From Danny -
(Today Danny is a successful entrepreneur, running several highly successful businesses.)

"When I was young, I was put in a school for retarded kids for two years before they realized I actually had a hearing loss...
and they call ME slow!"
Kathy Buckley

Sometimes it takes someone else to believe in you before you will believe in yourself. If you have limiting beliefs about yourself, you are restricted from creating the life you want and achieving all that you are capable of. You must never allow yourself and others to hold you back by feeding you limiting beliefs, which put a lid on your potential. Always remember that you become like the person you think and believe you are and you achieve only what you think and believe you are capable of achieving.

They are able because they think they are able.
Virgil

If you are told repeatedly that you are silly or stupid, you will eventually start to believe that you are and behave accordingly. This is why it is so important to start at a young age by encouraging children rather than criticising them, by promoting their strengths rather than focusing on their weaknesses and most of all by trying to sustain their belief in themselves. We all start out with a powerful belief in ourselves, which slowly becomes eroded by teachers, parents, friends, family and countless other influences. Protect this belief in yourself and in your children. Don't allow anyone or anything to tell you what you should or shouldn't believe, can or cannot do.

"Each second we live is a new and unique moment of the universe, a moment that will never be again...And what do we teach our children? We teach them that two and two make four, and that Paris is the capital of France.

When will we teach them what they are?

We should say to each of them: Do you know what you are? You are a marvel. You are unique. In all the years that have passed, there has never been another child like you. Your legs, your arms, your clever fingers, the way you move.

You may become a Shakespeare, a Michaelangelo, a Beethoven. You have the capacity for anything. Yes, you are a marvel. And when you grow up, can you then harm another who is, like you, a marvel?

You must work - we must all work - to make the world worthy of its children."

Pablo Casals

Awaken the Child Within

Sometimes I stop and take a good, hard look at myself
this person I've become.
Often I look too deeply and am shocked at what I find.
In a world of masks and facades, we lose ourselves.
Changing to suit the situation, acting out our part in the play of life.
We lose touch with reality and the real person
buried deep below is forgotten.
Some of us in our lifetimes will never reach deep enough
to unveil our true spirit.
Our true spirit and individuality, a gift from birth,
is often wasted and kept hidden from everyone's reach
and eventually from ourselves.
The child within is lost in an endless game of hide and seek.
Reach deep within yourself and find it.
Awaken your true spirit!
Awaken the child within, that child who can conquer the world!
Sally Eichhorst

I want you to start believing that you can do anything you truly put your mind to. It is a fact that if you believe you can, you will go to great lengths to prove yourself right. However, if you believe you can't, you will make a half-hearted attempt and will be doomed to failure before you have even begun. One of the main reasons why people do not succeed in life is because they do not believe they can. Yes, your beliefs about yourself and your capabilities are that powerful!

To enhance your self-esteem and confidence and thus create a belief in yourself, you must train yourself to think and speak positively about yourself and the world around you. You need to take a good look at what you are thinking about, listening to and speaking about all day long.

Maybe you are constantly thinking about everything that has gone wrong, is going wrong and could still go wrong in your life. To add to this possibly you are always speaking about the bad in the world and listening to one disaster story after the other. If this is the case, then be prepared to feel negative and down. Speaking about negative experiences and about the bad in the world is not going to make things better. Instead it will make you negative and depressed as you relive these unpleasant experiences and feel disillusioned with the world and life as a whole.

It might seem a little far-fetched to you, but it is a fact that what you see and hear all day has a definite influence on your state of mind. Even if you don't want it to effect you or don't think it is effecting you, subconsciously you react to it all. Unfortunately people love to tell and listen to disaster stories like violent crimes, horrendous accidents, accounts of other peoples' suffering and hardships. Maybe it makes them feel better about their lives, I don't know, but what I do know is that it has a negative outcome on their state of mind whether they like it or not.

The end result is that your beliefs will be negative and limiting, making you feel that there are no opportunities for improvement in your life and the world in general. This is bound to make you think and believe that you can't possibly prosper or achieve anything.

What you should be doing is thinking about all the positive things in your life, like: good memories, your achievements, your good qualities, your family and friends, exciting new opportunities and adventures that may lie ahead. You should also make sure that you speak positively not only about yourself but also about life and the world in general.

Rather focus on what's going right in the world at the moment and share some positive stories with people. Talk about good experiences you've had and what you still want to do with your life.

I just want to give you an example to verify what I've just said. My husband and I found that we would both become angry or upset when we read the paper or watched the news. Why? Because the news is filled mostly with disaster stories that horrify, upset and anger readers or viewers. Now we read the paper on rare occasions and watch the news only to catch the weather forecast at the end. Many may argue that we are turning a blind eye to what is going on or that we are losing touch with current events. My reply is that I see and hear about enough grief and hardship everyday and to supplement it further with page after page and story after story of violence, tragedy and mayhem seems senseless to me. I would rather focus on the good, positive aspects of life and to tell the truth I would rather only read the comic section of the paper for a good laugh. In fact we try never to miss a good laugh and when we do watch television, it's mostly only to watch the comedies so we can laugh at life and ourselves.

Now I want you to think carefully about the beliefs you have about yourself. If you have some powerful negative beliefs about yourself, like - 'I am a failure', 'I am not good enough', 'I am stupid' - I want you to write them down. Now look at them and ask yourself why you believe this to be true. Have others convinced you of this? Have certain actions or behaviour led you to believe this?

If other people have convinced you to believe something negative about yourself, then you have not protected your self-esteem and beliefs. You have allowed others to influence you negatively. Only you can decide what you will think and therefore believe. If others influence your thoughts and beliefs, it is because you have allowed them to. There comes a time in your life when you must choose your own thoughts and beliefs and accept responsibility for those choices. Be mature enough to believe what is right for you and not what others tell you to believe. Yes, you can choose to ignore what others tell you to think or believe and indeed you must if they are negative and only serve to break down your self-esteem and belief in yourself.

If certain of your actions or behaviour have resulted in negative beliefs about yourself, then you must analyse your reasoning. For example, if you believe you are stupid and cannot possibly be successful because you battled through school, then you are seriously misguided. Why? Because countless people who are certainly not stupid, battled in school and even left school with only a Std. 6 or Std. 8 pass only to become successful entrepreneurs, brilliant artists or outstanding athletes. Einstein himself was considered lazy and stupid at school and went on to become one of the scientific geniuses of all time. So, really think about why you believe these negative things about yourself. If it is an action or behaviour, which you can change, then work on changing it so that you may have a better image of yourself. Remember that being the person you want to be is a constant process.

If your negative belief about yourself is something you cannot change, then accept it and put it aside. Rather focus your energies on the things you can change for the better and at the same time celebrate and remind yourself constantly of the positive beliefs you have about yourself.

Do this now! Examine all the negative beliefs you have about yourself and work on transforming them to positive beliefs, which build you up rather than bring you down. For example change, 'I am a failure' to 'I always try my best' and 'I am not good enough' to 'I deserve the best'. I know you may think that this couldn't possibly have a positive effect on your life, but you're wrong. Your beliefs hold extreme power. They make up the person you become and greatly influence what you achieve in life. So it follows that changing your beliefs for the better can only change your life for the better.

The greatest discovery of my generation is that human beings can alter their lives by altering their attitudes of mind.
William James

Chapter 4

Making Good From Bad

Surfing Through Life!

Life is like surfing!
It's full of ups and downs.
When you're up, you're on the crest of a wave,
riding high with the wind in your hair and the feeling of freedom
and power in your veins.
When you're down, you've been dumped
and as the wave crashes over you,
it's like the world crashing down upon your shoulders
and you feel disoriented and vulnerable,
all dignity lost as you hit the deck.

So why surf?
Because the ups by far override the downs
and every time you're knocked down,
you learn a little more about how to stay up!

Sally Eichhorst

When I say to people that it is in their darkest hours that they often learn and grow the most, I am quite sure that many of them scoff and snigger unbelievingly to themselves. They just cannot comprehend that something good could possibly come of a "bad" experience or "mistake". I'll say it again, as I've said to numerous people, I don't believe in "mistakes", only lessons. I truly believe that we are constantly given lessons in life and this is why we never "know it all". These lessons come in various shapes and sizes to test us. If we do not learn the lesson, it is repeated in another form. The lesson often starts off easy and becomes harder the second time around. One thing is guaranteed, that lesson will be repeated again and again in different forms until it is learned.

"Often the very thing you think may bury you, can actually save you!"
Unknown

Only when one has learned the lesson, can one move on in life to better things. It is from the learning of these lessons that we grow in life and become stronger and more able to move on to new challenges. When people say to me that they feel "stuck", I believe that many of them are in fact unable to grow because they are unable to learn a vital lesson. They will remain "stuck" in their situation until they learn the lesson that life is trying to teach them. "Learn, let go and move on!" These words should be drummed into our heads from birth, as they are so important for our mental wellbeing.

Nothing is good or bad, but thinking makes it so.
William Shakespeare

As impossible as it sounds, the next time life seems to hand you a rotten tomato and you start thinking, "Why me?" rather change your thinking and ask yourself, "What can I learn from this?" or "How can I make this work for me instead of against me?" If you simply change the way in which you see and think about things, you can change a "bad" situation into a good one.

LET ME GIVE YOU A CLASSIC EXAMPLE.

This is an ancient story originating from the heart of Africa about the King of the Jungle - the Lion.

It was said that many years ago, a white Lion cub was born - the first of its kind! It attracted a great deal of curiosity and attention because it was so different and extraordinary. The local tribesmen heard about this rare entity and many "campfire" stories sprang to life, sparked by superstition and fear of the unknown.

One day a small group of herdsmen were drawn to the edge of a deep pit by a loud mewling sound. There at the bottom of the pit, unhurt, but desperately trying to claw its way up and out was the white Lion cub. They had heard so many conflicting stories about the creature and were unsure of what to do. After much heated discussion, they decided that they could not possibly get the cub out and it was therefore their duty to put the animal out of its misery by burying it in the pit.

So all the herdsmen busied themselves shoveling dirt steadily into the pit. To their amazement, the cub would shrug off the dirt as it fell on him and step up on top of it. He repeated this action with every shovel of dirt that fell on him. He would calmly shrug it off and step up on top of it.

Eventually the dirt had sufficiently filled the pit and it was built up high enough for the cub to jump triumphantly and unhurt to safety. The baffled and awe-struck herdsmen watched wide-eyed as the magnificent young creature turned to give them a long and penetrating parting look before bounding off to freedom.

The story of the white Lion cub's bravery and foresight spread far and wide. What was in fact supposed to bury it had actually saved it, all because of the way in which it had reacted to the situation. Instead of panicking and resigning itself to the fact that the dirt would bury it alive, it used the dirt to its advantage, building up a stepping stone for its escape.

And so the mystery of the great white Lion began. Today they are still a rare and magnificent sight and are symbolic of a positive omen because of the original white Lion cub's ingenious ability to make good of bad.

You too can make good of bad. As impossible as it sounds, everything in life happens for a reason. Even if the reason is not clear, sometimes we just have to accept, learn and move on.

EVERYTHING IN LIFE HAPPENS FOR A REASON

Accept that some days you're the pigeon
and some days you're the statue.

Author unknown

It was an ordinary and peaceful Sunday morning filled with delightful childish laughter and high-spirited fun and games. Angela was in the kitchen washing the breakfast dishes and watching the playful scene through the window. Her husband Tim was lounging on his favourite chair, lazily reading the Sunday paper whilst the girls were happily frolicking around him on the front lawn. Although they were both 4 years old, Carol was a lot smaller and frailer than her daughter Emily. They had become firm and fast friends since they had met at nursery school a year earlier. Carol was born with heart problems and Emily was always terribly protective over her sickly friend whom she loved dearly. Angela watched them fondly and never once did she imagine that this blissfully happy scene could change in an instant with tragic consequences, which would alter her life forever.

It all happened so fast. All Angela remembers is looking away for a second to pack away some dishes and when she looked back she could clearly see what was going to happen as if it were in slow motion, yet it was over before she heard herself scream.

Tim died in her arms as she knelt on the roadside with his head in her lap, mindlessly rocking him and moaning in her own private pain. A part of her died as he took his last breath and she felt her heart tearing into two. Carol was being examined by onlookers, but seemed to have suffered only some minor bruises and scratches. Angela felt instantly guilty as she thought it but she couldn't help thinking, 'Why? Why should my love die so that she who is already so sickly and may die any day soon can live? Why did he risk his life for someone else's child and rob his only child of a father? Why?'

It's the age-old story of ball bounces into road and little girl chases after ball. Only in this case a bus happened to be speeding past at exactly the same time and the girl's best friend's father reacts instinctively, racing to save her. Angela saw her Tim leaping into the road like a man possessed and sensing that there was no time to save them both, he hurled the screaming Carol to the safety of the curb as the bus came crashing down upon him.

10 years later Angela still could not accept Tim's death. Why did he allow himself to be killed to save someone else's child, especially a child who had a life threatening heart ailment from birth and was not expected to live long? She was bitter and angry at Tim for making that choice because it meant leaving her and his daughter Emily to live life without him. Yet she was also proud of his selfless act of heroism, which only made her love him and miss him more. However, she just could not let go of the nagging feeling that it wasn't fair. He shouldn't have lost his life over this. She simply could not accept that it was meant to be.

Then Angela's daughter Emily was diagnosed with an eye disease. She was told that unless a donor could be found, Emily would be left blind - blind at age 14; it was simply unthinkable and outrageously unfair! Then a miracle happened and it seemed that there was indeed an answer to all her questions and a reason behind everything in life.

At exactly the same time that Emily was diagnosed with this eye disease, her friend Carol, whom Tim had saved all those years ago, was dying from her lifelong heart ailment. Upon her death, Carol's corneas were donated to her friend Emily.

In dying to save Carol, Tim had unknowingly saved his own daughter from blindness later on in life. Angela now understands that everything in life happens for a reason. One simply has to accept it and let go. It has taken Angela a long time to understand and accept Tim's death, but in doing so she has learnt a lesson that takes most people a lifetime to realize and she feels she is a better person for it.

We have no right to ask when a sorrow comes, "Why did this happen to me?" unless we ask the same question for every joy that comes our way.
Philip F. Bernstein

Chapter 5

The Quest For Happiness

Happiness

A smile can win over friends and enemies alike.
Laughter can heal from within and spread warmth all about.
A friendly face is never a waste
and is always in good taste.
A helping hand
is someone who understands.
All in all, this is someone who has come to know,
that happiness is a self-created inward and outward glow.
It is not having the best of everything,
but rather making the best of everything and anything.

Sally Eichhorst

ANNIE'S STORY

The happiest people don't necessarily have the best of everything,
they just make the best of everything!

Sally Eichhorst

The entire ward was filled with patients suffering from depression. Most had arrived after suffering nervous breakdowns. As a social worker in training, it was part of my job to walk around and chat to all of them, not as a Psychologist, but rather as a friend. I was someone for them to talk to, who could sympathize and listen, but not advise.

I couldn't believe the vast number of people suffering from depression. I was really stunned and saddened by what I saw. I slowly made my way from patient to patient, spending only a brief moment with those who were too 'drugged up' to even notice me, but lingering on with others who were more clear-headed and seemed to need the company.

During my visits I learnt a great deal from the patients. Not that I pushed them for information - I was more like a sounding board to whom they volunteered information. With time, as patients came and went, what struck me most was that the majority of them seemed to have so much going for them.

Most of them were not clinically depressed, which would require constant medication to adjust a chemical imbalance, and none of them had a serious illness or disability. Many of these people were simply unhappy not unhappy due to losing a loved one or some other major traumatic event, but just unhappy about Life in general. When I chatted to many of them, they couldn't even pin point exactly what was causing the depression.

Some of them were just working too hard and had hit rock-bottom due to stress. Others were desperately lonely. Many were simply unhappy with their lives at home or work. Then there were those who were terribly dissatisfied with themselves, physically or mentally. One or two complained of serious financial problems and their inability to cope with life.

But on the most part, many of those I spoke to seemed to be pretty successful. They had just about everything they wanted and life should have been rewarding, yet here they were, in a mental ward. Call me the crazy one, but I just didn't understand it.

Then on one of my trips to the hospital, I accidentally stepped off the elevator on the wrong floor. Before I realized my mistake the doors closed and I was forced to wait for another elevator. Whilst waiting impatiently, I became aware of the sound of loud, free-spirited laughter.

Not just one, but many voices chuckling in a chorus of unashamed delight. What a welcome sound, compared to the sobbing and moaning associated with my usual visits upstairs. I simply couldn't resist finding out what all the laughter was about. Perhaps it would even put a much-needed smile on my face before I dealt with the depressed state of affairs upstairs.

A group of nurses, doctors and patients were crowded into one of the rooms and this was clearly from where the laughter emanated. I squeezed my way through the chuckling mass and when I saw the object of everyone's attention, I too was consumed with uncontrollable laughter.

A 'lucky legs' competition with a difference was being held. The legs in question were different in that none of them were human. There was a human being trying them on for size and attempting to sway his hips in a seductive-like wobble to show off the various leg options. While he was wobbling along unsteadily he gave a humorous rundown of all the features of the current leg on show - whether it was wooden, plastic, well shaped and life-like or easily adjustable and removable.

Confused? Well I was also momentarily confused until I noticed that all the patients who occupied beds in this room had one or two missing legs. The 'model' entertaining everyone with his antics had no right leg, yet he was parading around, joking about his situation and going to great lengths to make everyone laugh. His fellow patients were obviously delighted and screeched with laughter until their eyes were moist with laughter.

During the next few days I always made a point of popping in to see Tommy at the hospital before I went on to the depression ward. Tommy was the mischievous 'model' who had so thoroughly entertained everyone with his 'lucky legs' competition. He had recently lost his right leg in a motor car accident, yet one would think he had gained another leg, the way he carried on like things had never been better.

I was overwhelmed by Tommy's ability to constantly make the most of anything or any situation. By most standards, Tommy was a poor man who barely earned enough to support his family. He lived in a small flat with his wife and three children. They had only life's bare essentials, yet one would think they had it all, so happy were they. Even Tommy's accident could not put a damper on his spirits. He was happy to be alive and felt lucky to have come away with only a missing leg. 'Just think, my wife and children could have been with me in the car. I am so happy and thankful that they were not' he told me, winking knowingly at his wife who obviously adored him.

> *The wealthy man is the man who is much,*
> *not the one who has much.*

> **Karl Marx**

Indeed, Tommy was admittedly one of the happiest people I have ever had the pleasure of meeting and it was he who helped me to understand what I simply could not grasp before:

"The happiest people don't necessarily have the best of everything, they just make the best of everything."

It's amazing how many people suffer from regular bouts of depression. What's even more amazing is Annie's discovery that most of these unhappy people actually have so much going for them. So many people are desperately unhappy with their lives, when in fact they have little or no reason to be. The truth is, they should actually be celebrating the fact that they've got it so good.

> *A rich, full life is not determined by outer circumstances and*
> *relationships. These can be contributory to it, but cannot be the*
> *source. I am happy or unhappy because of what I think and feel.*

> **Unknown**

Unless you have a valid reason for suffering from depression like a chemical imbalance, which requires medication or you have recently experienced something traumatic, then your depression is more often than not a case of disillusionment with your life. Many depressed people are just disillusioned with their lives barring those individuals who have an understandable reason. It's all a matter of your frame of mind and the thoughts you dwell on. If you're going to think miserable and negative thoughts all day long, constantly seeing the negative side of things, you are creating a depressed person, no matter who you are and what riches and joys you may have in your life.

> *Most folks are as happy as they make up their minds to be.*
> **Abraham Lincoln**

You can choose to be happy or depressed no matter what your situation. Life is truly what you make of it. By making the most of what you have and focusing on the positives, you can see the brighter side of life and enjoy it to the full instead of becoming disillusioned with it.

This reminds me of a wonderful story about identical twins. Ask yourself which twin reminds you of yourself...

THE TWINS

There were identical twins in an orphanage. At 5 years of age their personalities were clearly beginning to shine through. One was said to be 'not so bright but jolly' and the other was described as 'serious, contemplative and intelligent'. Most potential adoptive parents were attracted to the description of the 'intelligent' child and wanted nothing to do with the 'not so bright but jolly' child. However the orphanage had a strict rule concerning twins - they must be adopted together.

One day a young couple visited the orphanage, keen to adopt a child of about the twins' age. They only wanted one child, but agreed to take the twins for the weekend as a trial period.

When they returned at the end of the weekend, they repeated what the orphanage had heard on numerous occasions. They really only wanted the one twin.

"Yes, yes I know you want the 'serious, contemplative and intelligent' twin, but I'm afraid they are a pair and must go together," said the House Mother regretfully.

"No, I think you misunderstood us," said the eager young couple. "We are interested in the 'bright and jolly' one. In fact, we like him so much that we are considering taking them both in the hope that the one becomes more like the other."

Confused, the House Mother tried to explain that they must have mixed up the two. One was indeed bright, yet more earnest, whilst the other was found to be less intelligent, yet full of cheer. There was no 'bright and jolly' twin.

"I'll give you an example," she told them. "Last year the boys were given welfare toys for Christmas. Being welfare toys, many of them were broken and unusable. One twin had the intellect to notice that they were broken and complained about it, while the other did not even seem to notice and played with them regardless, giggling as he pushed around the 'remote control' car, which had no remote and was missing a wheel! And just last week, we were all out walking when we came across a huge pile of manure. The 'intelligent' twin immediately wrinkled up his nose with distaste and disgust and announced 'Yuck, look at all that stinking manure!' At the same time the other one jumped up and down excitedly landing in the middle of the manure and gleefully throwing it up in the air while shouting happily 'Ponies, ponies, ponies!'

"Well, that's just it Mrs. Buckley," the young couple smiled knowingly at her. "It's you that's got it all wrong."

"What in the world are you talking about?" exclaimed Mrs. Buckley.

"You see, we've found that both twins are actually very bright. The only difference is that one is a hope-filled optimist and the other is a sad pessimist. The one you refer to as 'not so bright, but jolly' is in fact very bright and to put the cherry on top he's optimistic as well."

Seeing the puzzled look on Mrs. Buckley's face they went on to explain, "Your examples explain it perfectly. When the boys got broken welfare toys for Christmas, the optimistic twin knew they were broken, but he played with them regardless, making the most of an unhappy situation. He was just grateful to get something, whether it was broken or not. He played with that broken car all year, eventually replacing the broken wheel with one he found. In the meantime his twin refused to play with his broken toy truck, spending the year moaning and sulking about it.

And last week's incident with the manure is yet another example of the one twin's optimism and intelligence. While his twin saw the "yucky" side of the manure, associating it with something dirty, smelly and horrible, his optimistic brother associated it with lovely ponies, which all children adore. He had the intelligence to put the two together and grew really excited and happy at the thought of seeing the ponies. Surely you now understand why he's such a special child. Optimism is a quality we cherish, as should you. This boy has tons of it.

He's all that we could have hoped for in a son. He sees the bright side of everything, often reminding us to do the same. We just hope that his optimism rubs off a little on his twin. We'd like to adopt them both."

And so it is with all things in life. You can choose to see the good or bad side of every situation. Be very careful how you choose, for you may spend your life as a sad and hopeless pessimist who cannot recognize a good thing even when it lands on your lap. Remember, it is not the situation or experience which has value, you give it value by how you react to it. The same thing could happen to ten people and each of them could react completely differently. Some may overreact and cause great stress and emotional damage to themselves and others will blame and curse. Then there are those few, who will choose to look on the bright side by learning from what happened or seeing the good in it and moving on.

Trust me, choosing to see the bright side of things is a gift. Not many of us are lucky enough to be born as optimists. So we must develop this skill because life as a pessimist is a dull and bitter battle with no winners, for nothing can make a pessimist happy, except to fulfill his own prophesies of doom, gloom and destruction.

I challenge you to practice optimism. Honestly, I want you to start from this moment to try and see the bright and positive side of everything that you see, do, hear and experience. Force yourself to do this again and again. For some of you this will mean a radical change in your usual reactions, but stick with it. You see, the way we choose to react to things often becomes a habit like any other habit we develop through repetition. By constantly choosing to react optimistically, you will eventually fall into the habit of naturally seeing the good and positive side of everything. Come on, try it! It can only do you good!

Optimism builds character.
Pessimism destroys it.
So to build a life you must choose Optimism.

Sally Eichhorst

Chapter 6

Being All That You Can Be Through Mind Work

Only those who dare to fail greatly can ever achieve greatly.
Robert F. Kennedy

All the previous chapters of this book have dealt with adopting the right frame of mind. This is what mind work is all about. The fact is that without a positive frame of mind you are unlikely to achieve much. Therefore you must work on creating a positive mental attitude before you even begin to attempt achieving anything in life.

To give you an example, I'd like to discuss someone I know. This man is always complaining about not being able to succeed at anything. One day I sat down with him and together we went about trying to solve the mystery of his constant failure or inability to achieve his goals.

Firstly I told him to come up with some business ideas that interested him. At first he couldn't even do this. He was so negative, that when an idea popped into his mind he would dispel it seconds later before even voicing it. I could actually see him come up with an idea, his eyes sparkling with interest for a second or two and then before he could even mention it, the spark had gone as his negativity had already convinced him that it was impossible for him to achieve.

When he did eventually come up with one or two ideas, I was

thrilled, as I thought we had made a breakthrough. But when we started to discuss these ideas it only reconfirmed what I had suspected all along, that he was failing because of his negative frame of mind.

He ripped the ideas apart making hundreds of excuses why they would never work and why he couldn't do it. Not one positive thing came out of his mouth. He had literally convinced himself before he even began that it would fail. There was almost no doubt in his mind that every conceivable idea of his was impossible to achieve. Believe me when I say that his ideas were realistic and achievable, but not with his frame of mind and attitude.

Because he is a pessimist, this man is his own worst enemy. He is negative about everything and therefore attracts failure. He goes out of his way to look for the negatives in everything and consequently finds them or they find him.

To make things worse, someone with a negative frame of mind, is usually also negative about themselves. They often lack self-confidence and a belief in themselves. My friend is exactly like this. Not only does his negativity affect his belief about his goals, but also his belief about himself and his ability to achieve his goals.

As discussed in Chapter 3 of this book, an important area to work on is your beliefs about yourself and everything and everyone around you. Belief is a powerful thing. It is a fact that if you believe you can't, you can't. If on the other hand you believe you can, you can. People have achieved amazing and once thought impossible things, only because they first believed they could.

Now you see how important it is to do some "Mind Work" before you even attempt to achieve your goals and dreams in life. If you do not work on getting your mind right first, you are destined to fail before you even begin.

Stop moaning about those 'fat cats' on easy street who have achieved something. Instead of moaning about how lucky they are and how unfair it is, why don't you think about how they got there. More often than not, luck had absolutely nothing to do with it. They probably went out of their way to look for opportunities, often taking major risks, sacrificing a great amount of time and energy and really working for what they wanted. Now instead of sitting back and bemoaning your fate, why don't you change your attitude and look at what you can do to achieve the things you want. Stop focusing your mind on what you don't have and rather concentrate on what you do have and what you still want to achieve.

Goals are not only absolutely necessary to motivate us.
They are essential to really keep us alive.

Robert Schuller

YOU CAN BE LIKE HIM!

Remember the story of the ugly duckling? Well, I have a similar story to tell you. The story begins in very much the same way, with a swan's egg accidentally being misplaced and landing among those of an unsuspecting duck.

The swan hatches with the ducklings and grows up with them. All it's life, the swan believes it is a duck and therefore it behaves like a duck, attempts to quack like a duck, associates only with ducks and eats only what they eat.

Many years pass by and the swan grows old and tired. Deep down, he has always felt that he is somehow different. He always dreamed that there was more to his life and that he was meant for bigger and better things.

One day, he saw the most magnificent and beautiful bird he had ever seen before. It seemed to dance above the lake before landing gracefully and ever so gently upon the water. It's head was held up high and proud on a long and slender neck as it glided effortlessly through the water.

"Oh, what a lovely bird. I've never seen anything so beautiful and majestic! I can't imagine what it could be?" wondered the old swan in awe.

"That's a swan; the most beautiful and graceful of all the birds," quacked one of his fellow ducks. "But don't you get any ideas. Accept that you're just a duck. You could never be like him!"

So the old swan resigned himself to the fact that he was just a duck and an ugly one at that. He accepted that he could never even hope to be anything remotely like the beautiful and majestic swan he had seen.

So he never thought about it again and he died thinking he was only an ugly duck.

You see, you are what you think! You too could be a swan who thinks it's only a duck. The truth is you can be anything you want to be. You can be like someone you admire and respect. If you think you're meant for bigger and better things, then go out there and pursue them. Don't settle for second best. You can be all that you want to be if you get your mind right!

You create your own pot of gold at the end of the rainbow.

Sally Eichhorst

Before continuing on to Part 2.
I want you to always remember that the task ahead of you is never as great as the power within you.

Part 2

Character Work

You Are Unique

You may not think that the world needs you, but it does.
For you are unique, like no one that has ever been
before or will come after.
No one can speak with your voice, say your piece, smile your smile,
or shine your light.
No one can take your place, for it is yours alone to fill.
If you are not there to shine your light,
who knows how many travelers will lose their way
as they try to pass by your empty place in the darkness?

Author unknown

Chapter 7

Never Lose Hope

Of all the people you will know in a lifetime, you are the only one you will never leave nor lose, therefore it is essential to like yourself, find yourself acceptable, worthy of respect, admiration and love.

Sally Eichhorst

I recently met with a very disturbed and broken spirit. For me, one of the saddest things to witness is a person who has lost respect and value for themselves, believing with time that they deserve to be treated with total disregard as though their existence is meaningless and worthless.

She sat before me apologizing constantly for one thing after the other. At first it was for her appearance, then for her behaviour and eventually she even apologized for opening up to me and sharing her problems with me and she was sorry for taking up and wasting so much of my precious time.

This poor lady seemed to think that she owed the world an apology for merely existing. I wanted so badly to prove her wrong and from the outset I encouraged her to stop apologizing when there was absolutely nothing for her to apologize about.

Severe emotional abuse and a little physical abuse to boot, had slowly worn down her self-esteem, leaving a nearly empty shell of the once confident and secure person she had been. Trapped in a marriage due to financial constraints and treated like dirt by her husband as well as her children, who had also lost respect for what had become a weak and spineless slave to fetch and carry, pick up and clean after them. Her opinion didn't count in her own home. Her own home had become a prison where she was confined by the need for money to survive. She hadn't worked for years and had minimal experience and therefore no opportunities in an already battered economy with ever-increasing unemployment rates. So she felt stuck, trapped in this life for the time being and every day that she remained there, she was losing just a little more of her self-worth and self-confidence.

She told me that she had been given advice by someone recently and asked my opinion. She was told as so many of us are again and again throughout our lives by well-meaning people trying to sound wise and all-knowing that 'She must be realistic as life is not a bed of roses. The real world is full of thorns - bad people, the constant need for money, hurt, abuse, heartache and loss and she must just accept that this is life.'

'What do you believe?' I had asked her. She'd replied, 'Yes, I believe the world to be an ugly and cruel place!' She gave me a long list to back up her argument, but I had sensed that she desperately wanted and even needed me to prove her wrong.

'So what do you believe?' she'd asked me.

'I believe in the value of all people and all things. I believe that although life may not always be a bed of roses, the beauty and lingering good of the roses outweigh all the thorns. I believe in being optimistic rather than realistic. I'm not saying walk around with your head in the clouds with a constant silly grin plastered on your face. What I'm trying to say, is that we all know the reality of crime, violence, heartache and all the other negativity in the world, so why make it worse by focusing on it? Rather focus on the positives of the world and in your life. If there aren't many good things in your life, then start taking positive action, no matter how small to change your situation. Realize that you don't have to be forced into becoming a 'realist', becoming bitter and twisted as you review all the negatives in your life and the world around you. There are still good people who care - There are still those who save lives rather than take them - Those who give rather than steal - Those who protect and shelter rather than abuse - Those who love rather than hate. Sure life can sometimes be cruel and unkind, but never forget that it can also be extraordinarily beautiful. Most importantly, I believe that life is full of hope for a better tomorrow and I believe that there is hope for you.'

'Do you really think I could change my life? Do you think I could do better? I used to think I deserved better, but I'm not so sure anymore.' She'd said shyly.

'That's where you'll have to start then' I remember saying. 'Your first positive step to changing your life for the better will be to get your mind right. Of course you deserve better - everyone deserves to be treated with respect and to be valued, but first you must learn to value yourself again. Focus on your positive qualities and refuse to be treated disrespectfully. Learn to value yourself and soon others will value you more too. The self-confidence and self-worth you gain will help you to build a new life and help you to realize that there are options, rather than shackles, hope rather than fear and despair.'

When she had left, there was a new sparkle of life in her eyes and a new spring in her step. I saw a wonderful smile that lit up her entire face and most importantly I saw a hint of the self-confident and self-assured person that had once been. Yes, there is hope for her and for everyone who deserves a better life. It's never too late to rebuild your life. Just start somewhere. Every small positive action will generate a small positive result and eventually a better and more deserving life. There is always hope!

Don't undermine your worth by comparing yourself with others. It is because we are different that each of us is special.
A Creed To Live By Nancye Sims

In a world that seems to be a money-hungry jungle, where only the strong or bad survive, where cruelty, hardship and outrageous atrocities are becoming more and more common place, many have become victims of bitterness and despair. Don't allow all this negativity to steal your chance at a happy life. Some say it's being realistic to harp on the negatives and injustices of the world, becoming bitter and disillusioned as a result. Some believe there is no good left in the world, but I know they're wrong. I look around me every day and I see hope. Believe it or not, in this troubled world of ours, there are still those that care. As long as there are good people around and there is beauty to behold, then there is always hope. Hope that the world can be a better place and that the good still outweighs the bad. Hope that there will always be more positives in our lives than negatives if only we choose to see them and cherish them. Hope is only dead when you allow it to be…

Chapter 8

Giving Is Better Than Receiving

The wheel of life keeps turning so what you give or take will eventually come back to you. Make sure you look forward to its arrival.

Sally Eichhorst

KINDNESS IS THE OIL THAT TAKES THE FRICTION OUT OF LIFE!

I was looking forward to the movie as we stood in a long queue of people eagerly anticipating the promise of superb entertainment. I was only a late blooming teenager then, going to watch an afternoon show with my Mom. We were both big sentimental 'softies' and loved a good heart warming movie with meaning and depth.

We were quite intrigued by a frail old, grey-haired granny dressed in her Sunday best with a horde of little children in tow. They were ahead of us in the queue and we were amazed at how well behaved the little ones were. There were six of them. Four girls and two boys, all ranging in age from about 5 to 10 years old. I immediately sensed that they were not very well off as their clothing, although it may have been their Sunday best, was old, faded and ill-fitting. Yet they were all clean-scrubbed and impeccably behaved and stood in a straight line behind the old lady, whispering excitedly to one another and giggling happily with nervous anticipation.

The grey-haired granny smiled warmly down at the children. One could clearly see that the children adored her and looked up to her. It was also obvious that this was a rare treat for them and I was sure that it might possibly even be their first time at a movie theatre.

The old granny looked as though she was bubbling over with love for them and almost bursting at the seams with pride.

It was her turn at the front of the queue and she shuffled forward slowly, standing as straight and proud as can be and beaming happily at the ticket operator.

"These are my six grandchildren. I haven't seen them for some time as they live far away in the countryside. They've never been to a real live movie you see. I promised them a day they'd never forget. We're all really excited and ..."

"Yes, yes. That's lovely" interrupted the ticket operator. He was tired and irritable and had no time to listen to a little old lady rambling on about her life. He had work to do and a long queue still waiting. "How many tickets and what show?" he asked trying unsuccessfully to conceal his impatience.

"I need six tickets for children and one for an adult to see 'Lady and the Tramp'" she said confidently with her head held high and her purse clasped firmly to her chest as she awaited his response.

"That will be R46.00 altogether" announced the ticket operator, smiling falsely through gritted teeth as he glanced at the growing queue behind her.

It was clear to me that this total came as a shock to the little old granny. Her confident smile vanished and her face became pale and then flushed as she blushed with embarrassment. She then searched feverishly in her purse for the extra money, which she knew she did not have. She obviously hadn't been to the movies herself in years and had never imagined that the prices could have increased to such an extent.

I shuffled uncomfortably from foot to foot, feeling somehow awkward and embarrassed for her. Her shoulders seemed to droop resignedly and she hung her head undecided, as she looked at the six tiny and hopeful faces gazing expectantly up at her.

Just then I noticed my Mom reaching quietly into her own purse so no one would notice and pulling out two twenties. She then dropped them on the floor, undetected (except by me!) and leaned forward, tapping the frail old shoulder before her. "Excuse me, my dear, I think you dropped some of your money," said my Mom warmly as she squeezed the old lady's arm affectionately.

The old granny understood perfectly well what had happened and fought back a tear as she whispered gratefully, "Thank you. Thank you so much for noticing. My grandchildren and I are really grateful." She picked up the R40.00 from the floor and paid the balance from her purse. My Mom and her exchanged one last knowing look before she marched her excited little brood into the movie theatre.

That was the last we saw of them for although we were next in line, Mom suddenly said that she wasn't feeling so well and would prefer to go home. We could always see the movie another time.

She never did admit that the real reason we had left was because she had given away all the money she had in her purse to the little old granny. Mom was by no means wealthy, but what she lacked in financial matters she made up for in matters of the heart. She had sacrificed a little so that someone else could gain a lot. She was indeed a big 'softie' and no movie could ever have left me feeling as warm, proud and hopeful in the good nature and spirit of mankind as this experience had.

> *The best portion of a good man's life - his little, nameless,*
> *un-remembered acts of kindness and love.*
> **William Wordsworth**

In a world that so often makes us fear that mankind has lost its ability to be humane, it is so refreshing to witness or indulge in moments of kindness. Indeed, kindness is the oil that takes the friction out of life. You've really got to try it sometime! It's a healthy rush!

WORK ON THE ART OF GIVING...

I was driving along in my car the other day becoming increasingly irritable with the traffic jam I found myself in. I decided to turn up the radio as a distraction and my mood changed instantly when I tuned in to this wonderful program about the joys of giving. Listeners are urged to contact the radio station with a request for someone in need or even for someone who simply deserves some sort of recognition or reward for their actions.

On this particular day, a request had been made by the family of a very ill lady, who was in desperate need of a double lung transplant. Her medical expenses were exorbitant and her family was battling to cope. She also needed a wheelchair and many other bits and pieces to help keep her comfortable during the long wait for a possible donor.

I was touched when they interviewed her family and moved to tears when listeners who were in a position to help offered their services and products for free. A pharmacy offered to pay for all her medication. An oxygen supplier said they would supply her with free oxygen. A wheelchair was given to the family for as long as they needed it and then a plea was made to all listeners to give the greatest gift of all to become a donor in the event of death so that they may save the life of another.

It really did my heart good to know that there are still so many kind, generous and caring people left in the world. I am so glad that the art of giving has not yet become extinct. I call it an art because it is truly a beautiful thing. It means different things to different people and releases all sorts of emotions, creating a warmth from within. Try it sometime! Give from the heart without expecting anything in return. It is indeed one of life's great joys to witness the happiness and appreciation you can create by giving.

Blood donors and organ donors are giving the greatest gift of all - the gift of life! However there are many more ways for you to give of yourself. You can give an old person that you know assistance by offering to run some errands for them. You can volunteer some of your time to help a charity organization or you can make small donations whenever you can to one or more charities. Remember that giving of yourself does not always mean financially. Think about ways in which you may be able to give your time, expertise, companionship and support to others - I assure you there are always plenty of people who need it.

I believe firmly that giving is so much better than receiving. The joy you spread in giving stays with you for a long time, like a warm and satisfying glow. Maybe if more people actually practiced the art of giving instead of taking, the world would be a much happier and friendlier place.

I am also a great believer in what comes around goes around. So if you give freely without expecting anything in return, you will get back tenfold, when the time is right. - I remember reading in the Time magazine that only 100 people in the world are responsible for 75% of donations to charities worldwide so you can imagine how much each of these individuals must be contributing. They contribute millions without asking for anything in return. Many may argue that they can afford it because they are successful, but I strongly believe that part of their success is due to their generosity and willingness to help others who are not as fortunate. Many people including myself feel that the greatest thing that comes from success is to be able to use it to help family, friends and those in need. Yes, giving is better than receiving!

You do not have to be rich to be generous. If he has the spirit of true generosity, a pauper can give like a prince.

Corrine V. Wells

Chapter 9

True Beauty Shines Through From Within

Is it not sad that if only those who had something good to say were allowed to speak, there would be almost deathly silence in the world.

Sally Eichhorst

CHOOSING A PRINCESS

Many years ago in ancient times, there lived a very powerful and wise old King. His greatest joy was his bright and handsome son. The Prince was ready for marriage. It was the King's duty to choose the Prince's bride and he would settle for nothing less than the best for his beloved son.

The wise old King was well aware of the importance of choosing a bride who was not only beautiful in appearance, but more importantly also beautiful from within. That special someone would be wise beyond her years just as his wonderful late wife, the Queen had been.

The King pondered for many days in his study until at last he came to a decision. He decided to host a luncheon inviting all prospective ladies from far and wide. It would be a grand occasion with loads of entertainment, gallons of wine and a feast of food to satisfy even the fussiest palate.

There was great excitement throughout the land as all the ladies of class and standing received their invitation to the King's luncheon.

The Big day finally arrived and the castle was filled with the hustle and bustle of busy servants. The Hallway rang with the laughter and giggles of 20 young ladies, jostling one another for the King and Prince's attention. The massive dining room was alight with a cascade of colour from all the bright and eye-catching garments and the atmosphere was one of nervous excitement and expectancy.

Ladies smiled insincerely at one another through gritted teeth. There was much leering, sneering and backbiting as they sized up the competition. After all they were all here to compete for the Prince.

The King sat at the head of the table, quietly taking in the scene. The Prince sat on his right, looking a bit bewildered and overwhelmed by the whole event. Both Father and Son were like spectators at a cat fight, as they listened to one lady after the other voice her views and opinions. Sometimes they were forced to listen to two at a time as the ladies vied for attention, often interrupting one another or silencing the other mercilessly with sharp remarks and poisonous tongues.

Already the King had ruled out 10 of the prospects. Although beautiful in appearance and of good breeding, the King had already observed an ugliness about them. It was sad and bewildering that such young ladies were already so hardened and bitter. A wise man, such as the old King, was not fooled by the mask of beauty and class. He easily recognized the false smiles and never missed an ugly remark. Those who had nothing good to say about anyone or anything but themselves were certainly not fit to be a Princess.

After their huge lunch, the King invited the 10 young ladies he had short-listed to accompany him and his son on a short walk to help settle their food.

The ladies looked questioningly at one another as the King's stroll led them to the servants' quarters. To their amazement, the King invited them all inside. It was a hot summer's day and they were all a little thirsty. The King asked one of the maids to bring them each a glass of water.

The maid was young, inexperienced and taken aback by the unannounced visit. In her nervous state she spilled a great deal of the water from the glasses. A number of the young ladies complained bitterly at her clumsiness and others moaned that their glasses were now half empty.

The young maid blushed profusely and looked about to burst into tears when one of the ladies smiled brightly and said, 'Don't upset yourself, at least the glasses are still half full and we are able to quench our thirst thanks to you.' The maid smiled shyly at her with relief before turning away.

The King hadn't really noticed her before, for she was by far the plainest of all the ladies. Her dress was clean and formal, but certainly not eye catching or expensive. She wore no jewellery and barely a smudge of make-up. One of the ladies whispered in his ear like a conspirator, 'That's Elizabeth. She comes from up North. I'm not sure why she's even here. Her family are hardly of good breeding. I believe they are landowners, but barely scratch out a living. How she can be considered a lady, I don't know!'

The King immediately struck the 'ear whisperer' from his list of potential Princesses as well as all the ladies who had moaned at the young maid. That left only 5 to choose from.

The King asked the 5 ladies he had ruled out as candidates to leave and focused his attention on the 5 remaining ladies. 'I want you to tell me what you see when you look around you,' he said.

Almost all the answers were very similar and went something like this: 'I see dirty, smelly servants quarters', 'I see crammed, stuffy rooms filled with cheap things', 'I see poverty and unhygienic surroundings', and 'I see plain, unclean and undecorated rooms'.

Only one answer was remarkably different: 'I see poor, but decent hardworking people trying to make an honest living. I see clean rooms, sparsely decorated, but decorated with lovely, sentimental things. I see people who take pride in what little they have by looking after it.' Elizabeth looked at everyone apologetically as they all stared at her with disbelief and what she assumed to be disgust. 'I'm sorry, but that's what I see,' she said and blushed hotly at their disapproval.

The King was intrigued. There seemed to be a lot more to young

Elizabeth than met the eye. The closer he looked, the more lovely and appealing she seemed. How had he overlooked her so easily before, he wondered.

The King's thoughts were interrupted by a group of rowdy, playful children, falling all over one another at the door in an excited heap. 'Such noisy and unruly little brats,' said one of the ladies to the other. 'Oh, and look how ghastly and ill mannered they are,' remarked the other.

The King looked at Elizabeth to see her response. She had a bright smile on her face and was watching the children with pure delight. 'What do you think of this noisy bunch then Elizabeth?' he asked. 'I think they're wonderful! Look at them so full of life and fun, without a care in the world. I think we could all learn from them,' said Elizabeth while the other ladies again fixed her with disapproving stares.

The King had seen enough.

Princess Elizabeth was adored by everyone!

It took a wise King to see the beauty shining through from within. But why Elizabeth?

During the luncheon, Elizabeth never once said a nasty or critical word about anyone. She only spoke when she had something good to say.

She treated the maid who had spilled the water with respect regardless of her class. She recognized the maid's distress and came to her rescue even at the risk of disapproval from everyone else.

She saw the glass of water as half full, not half empty. The King recognized this as a sign of a positive person, who looks at the bright side of life and situations.

Elizabeth saw the good and beauty in everyone and everything, whether it was the servants quarters or a group of filthy, playful children. She loved children for she believed they had the right idea about life - LIVE IT TO THE FULL! BE ADVENTUROUS AND HAPPY. SEIZE THE MOMENT!

In all these ways, Elizabeth's true beauty shone through from within. **So can yours!**

Before you demand respect from others,
first make sure that you deserve the respect you desire.

Sally Eichhorst

I remember my husband and I discussing a wedding we had attended a day earlier and he spoke about a beautiful woman he had observed there. Trying to hide my annoyance and eliminate all hints of jealousy I cautiously asked, "What beautiful woman?" He immediately reassured me by naming the woman in question. She was certainly no threat as she was a friend's mother and I was puzzled as to why he thought she was a beautiful woman.

'I was just observing everyone and listening to them chatting in their little groups around the tables, when I noticed something very interesting,' explained my husband. 'Everyone seemed to be standing around gossiping, criticizing, telling disaster stories, moaning and groaning about the economy and the general state of the world. I was so delighted when I finally came across a positive person among all the doomsayers and critics. She was sitting with a large group of woman discussing various absent 'friends' when I heard her defending one of them. As I listened further I heard her come to the rescue of many others by pointing out their good points and reminding those present of the positives of all people. I sat for a long time listening to the conversation and not once did I hear her criticize, put down or say anything remotely nasty about anyone. Instead she seemed to genuinely see the good in everyone and everything, always pointing out the positives of the situation or the person in question. There was no falseness or ulterior motive for her kindness and consideration and she certainly did not come across as a weak minded or gullible person who believed only in the good of all people and things.

This was a lady who thought positively about herself, about her situation, about the people around her and about life in general. She was beautiful from the inside and this beauty seemed to shine through making an otherwise plain appearance seem extraordinarily beautiful.

Always keep your words soft and sweet,
just in case you have to eat them.

Author Unknown

I overheard someone chatting about her and they described her life as happy, successful, full of friends and complete. You see, a beautiful appearance eventually becomes ordinary the longer you behold it and will ultimately fade with time. But beauty from within is something extraordinary, which shines brighter over time and outlasts the person themselves.

Talk is cheap because supply exceeds demand!

Author Unknown

In a world so obsessed with and focused on outward appearance, we should rather concentrate our energies on becoming better people and creating a beautiful person from within so that we may one day look back and be proud of who we are and what we have said and done.

Think about what would make you a better person. Write down these thoughts. Do it right now! Read what you have written every day as a reminder to adjust your behaviour accordingly. In this way you need to train yourself to constantly strive and work towards being the person you want to be.

Why not try to give so much time to the improvement of yourself that
you have no time to criticize others?

C.D. Larson

Chapter 10

A Little Character Work Prevents A Lot Of Heartache

DON'T PLAY JUDGE

It was another blistering hot day outdoors and people had been streaming into the air- conditioned restaurant all day for relief from the heat and to quench their thirst.

Cindy had noticed the dirty little street urchin lurking about outside, offering to polish the shoes of passers-by with a cloth that looked decidedly filthier than the shoes it was supposed to clean. She was mildly irritated when she saw the boy push his way through the restaurant doors and seat himself at the counter.

She watched with distaste, as his grubby little fingers pawed the menu. She could just imagine all the germs and bacteria that would remain after his departure.

"Can I help you?" she asked the boy perhaps a little too harshly, unable to conceal her irritation. "How much are your milkshakes?" he inquired shyly. "Large milkshakes are R12.99, medium are R9.99 and the small one's are R4.50" she replied with increasing annoyance as she took in the smell of him and noticed the dirty finger imprints he was making all over the menu.

"Oh," said the boy disappointedly. "How much for a small coke then?" he asked hopefully. "That'll be R4," said Cindy impatiently, wondering why he was studying the menu at all when he obviously couldn't read it. "I'll have a small coke then," said the boy.

Cindy brought him the coke along with the bill and went to tend to her other clients. But she constantly watched the grubby little fellow out the corner of her eye as she expected him to run off any minute without paying the bill. He was probably waiting for her to look away so he could escape undetected and score a free coke, which she would then have to pay for out of her meagre salary and pathetic tips.

She was still spitting mad because the last table she had served, had been occupied by a group of wealthy-looking holiday makers and she had expected a good tip, only to find that they had left her not even 1 cent. Well, if this little street urchin thought he was going to cheat her out of money, he was going to be unpleasantly surprised.

To Cindy's dismay, she was called into the kitchen urgently as one of her orders had been misplaced. This meant that she would lose sight of the boy for awhile. As fate would have it, on her return, the boy was gone. She rushed to the door and looked out into the street, but there was no sign of him. Mumbling angrily to herself, she inspected the area where he had been sitting to make sure he hadn't stolen anything. Still cursing herself for serving him in the first place and not chasing him out immediately, she was stunned by what she found.

To Cindy's surprise, tucked neatly under the bill, she found exactly R4.50. R4 for the coke and 50c as a tip for her. Cindy blushed in shame, because not only did the boy pay in full, but he had sacrificed having a small milkshake, which cost exactly R4.50 and instead had a coke for R4 so that he could leave her a 50c tip.

Cindy was ashamed of her behaviour and overwhelmed by the boy's consideration and generosity. She had misjudged the little guy because of who he was and what he looked like. She wished she could turn back time to when he had pushed his way through the doors earlier. She would be so much kinder to him. Maybe she would even pay for his milkshake. For days Cindy waited for the boy to return.

That particular little boy never did come back, but many other shabby looking characters came and went through the doors and Cindy made it her mission to treat every one of them with kindness, respect and warmth. She'd learnt a very important lesson - 'Never judge a book by its cover.'

In life, we so often judge people unfairly and for the wrong reasons. Don't judge someone because of their status in life, for you may be joining them one day. Likewise don't judge people by their appearance as I've seen many a scoundrel dressed in gentleman's clothing. Also don't judge someone too soon on their behaviour. Perhaps if you were to walk in their shoes for a day, you would behave exactly the same.

If we had no faults,
we would not take so much pleasure in noting those of others.

Francoise de La Rochfoucauld

CONTROL YOUR ANGER AND GET YOUR PRIORITIES STRAIGHT!

A man had just bought himself an expensive new sports car. He was immensely proud of the car and all that it represented, success, status, quality, good taste and wealth. He looked after his new prize with a passion, cleaning, shining and polishing it to perfection. Not a speck of dust dared rest on his beautiful car. Indeed no one could dispute that it was in mint condition.

One day he entered his garage to begin his morning ritual of inspecting his car and polishing its already shiny exterior. To his horror, his young son was hard at work scrubbing the car with a wire brush, leaving deep and damaging scratches in the fine paint- work.

Understandably the man was furious. Always quick to react in anger, he flew into an uncontrollable rage. He grabbed the boy's hands, which had inflicted the damage to his most prized possession and pummelled them to a pulp. Only once he had calmed down, did he realise the extent of his son's injuries and immediately rushed him to the nearest hospital.

All of his son's little fingers had been smashed to a pulp, doing irreparable damage to the bones and leaving no other option for doctors, but amputation. All ten of the young boy's fingers were consequently amputated.

When the little guy awoke after surgery he immediately asked for his Daddy. "I'm sorry about your car Daddy. It was supposed to be a

Father's Day surprise. I wanted to finish cleaning it before you got there, but the more I scrubbed, the more marks I seemed to make. When will my fingers grow back so I can fix your car for you?" he asked innocently.

It was reported that neighbours were alarmed by a successful and well known businessman who upon returning home, proceeded to smash his prized new sports car to pieces with a baseball bat. A small crowd of bewildered onlookers had gathered and watched as the man repeatedly smashed his car while yelling again and again, "What was I thinking, the boy was my prize possession, not the car!"

This story disturbed me immensely, as it should you. For just a few minutes of anger, this man had lost a lifetime of happiness. His sports car could be fixed, but his son could not be. He would have to live with this for the rest of his life. And so it is with anger, which so often leaves a wound or scar that may never heal, doing irreparable damage.

Not only was this man guilty of lashing out in anger, but he was also just as guilty of losing sight of his priorities in life. Unfortunately, he realised this too late. His new sports car was great, but it was only a car made of cold, unfeeling metal, replaceable and with a price tag attached to it. But his son was his life, a warm, feeling part of him whom he loved and wouldn't sell for all the money in the world. His son was in fact the most valuable thing in his life, certainly not his car. How he must have hated that car afterwards, but not nearly as much as he hated himself.

I urge you to always think twice before resorting to anger. Think always of the consequences and the unnecessary damage you could cause to someone you love. Think about this story the next time you fly into a rage. Think before you act!

Have a good think about your priorities. What are they? Remember that if you get your priorities wrong, you stand a far greater chance of losing what is actually most important to you.

PRACTICE UNCONDITIONAL LOVE

It was the end of the Second World War and the world was still reeling with shock at the devastation that the war had left in its wake.

A young soldier, or more accurately a mere boy, was excited about returning home to the love of his parents and the comfort and security of a supportive family. He had seen and experienced too many terrible things for one so young. The war had aged him and very nearly broken his spirit. It was the knowledge that he was loved deeply and that his parents would be waiting for him with open arms that saved him from despair. They loved him and would be so proud of him and that was all that mattered. Their love would carry him through.

He excitedly called his parents to let them know he was coming home at last. "Mom and Dad, it's true, I'm finally coming home! I can hardly wait to see you both!" he exclaimed happily.

"Oh, that's wonderful news my boy," said his father warmly while his mother shed tears of relief and happiness.

"There's just one thing I need from you," said the young soldier worriedly.

"Anything son!" said his parents.

"I'd like to bring someone home with me. He's a friend who has nowhere to go and …"

"Well, of course you can. We'd love to meet him." his father cut in before he could finish.

"You didn't let me finish Dad. There's something you should know about my friend. He risked his life to save someone in our squad and he was badly injured. In fact, he's in pretty bad shape. He lost both legs and an arm and as I said he has nowhere else to go. I said he could come and live with us."

"That's just terrible Son. Sure we'd still love to meet him, but surely you can't expect us to take him in. Someone with such a serious handicap requires a great deal of attention and financial support. Such a seriously handicapped person would be a burden on us for the rest of our lives. As much as we'd love to help, it would just be too much of a strain on the family. I'm sure there are various charity organisations that may help him. Surely you can see and understand how it would interfere with our lives. Why don't you just come on home? I'm sure your friend will work something out. We just want our old son back ..."

The line suddenly went dead before the boy's father could finish his sentence.

The following day, the young soldier's parents received another call from the military headquarters abroad. Expecting to be re-connected to their son, they were a little startled to find his immediate superior on the line.

"I'm so sorry, your son died late last night. He was shot ..."

"Shot! What do you mean? The war is over. How could this have happened?" cried the distraught father.

"Sir, your son shot and killed himself. We are certain it was suicide." said the officer sadly.

The grieving parents were flown to the military headquarters to identify their son and claim his body.

Before they were taken to see him, their son's superior officer came to pay his condolences.

"I just wanted to let you know how brave your son was. Did he tell you that he risked his life to save a friend and was hurt very badly as a result? He seemed to be recovering so well and was truly an inspiration to us all. I don't know why he ended it like this? I really don't understand what went wrong?" he said emotionally.

When the parents saw their dead son, the mother fainted and the father had to be tranquillised. Their son was missing both legs and an arm. The 'friend' their son had spoken of, was in fact himself.

"Love and be loved unconditionally.
It's the only way!"

Chapter 11

Become A Better Person Through Character Work

To be conscious of no faults is indeed the greatest of all faults.

Unknown

Before moving on to the next part of this book I want you to take a long, hard look at yourself. Do you like what you see? I don't mean physically, I'm more concerned about what's inside that outer shell of yours - your character. We all have character flaws that we need to recognize and work on, some more so than others.

I know that many people will try to convince you that the good people of this world often get walked over, taken for granted, cheated and hurt. Please don't fall for this nonsense. Sure, people often do get hurt, trampled upon and cheated, but not necessarily because they're good, but rather because those that inflict the pain are not. If more people in this world were of good character, there would certainly be a lot less hurt, disappointment and pain in the world.

It's not easy to change a bad habit or character trait, but it is possible if you really want to make the effort. No one can make you change. It has to come from you. In the same respect, you cannot change someone else - they must want to change. I've come across so many couples who got married thinking that they could change their partner over time. I don't think so! Unless that person wants to change, that bad habit or character trait, which you detest, will just become more ingrained. Forget about trying to change others! That's their job. Rather concentrate on changing yourself for the better.

Character work is a constant process, which will never be fully complete in your lifetime as there is always more to learn and do. Keep at it!

So how does working on your character help you to live the life of your dreams? Well, it makes you more likeable and approachable, therefore opening many doors and attracting people and opportunities to you. It's an obvious fact that people would rather deal with and help someone they like and trust.

Furthermore as I touched on earlier in 'Giving is better than receiving', the wheel of fortune keeps turning and I firmly believe that what goes around, comes around. So if you are kind and helpful and essentially good without expecting anything in return, you will receive everything back tenfold.

Part 3

Dream Work

Allow yourself to dream

*Allow yourself to dream
and to dream big!
Allow yourself to wonder at what could be
and to ponder at the vast possibilities.
Allow just a moment in Time to imagine the joy of living your dream
and to know that you can do it.
Allow yourself to dream
and never to lose sight of what may be,
for people without dreams, don't have much.*

Sally Eichhorst

Chapter 12

My Lovely Ordinary Life!

The secret of life isn't what happens to you and what you have, but what you do with what happens to you and how much you appreciate what you have.

Author unknown

So what makes you or me an ordinary person? What constitutes an ordinary life? Is ordinary good or bad? Does it make you boring or more acceptable?

These are questions I asked myself today as I thought about my life. Sometimes we get to a stage where we take a close look at our lives and find ourselves faced with the image of an everyday person, making a regular living, married to yet another everyday person and living in an unremarkable house with set routines and daily habits. Over time, it all becomes ordinary and perhaps we wake up one day thinking - 'So, is this what life's all about? Am I missing something or is my life just dull and unspectacular? Am I ordinary and unremarkable? Should I change my situation by doing some wild and abnormal things? What about changing my line of work or looking for some other exciting distraction to make my life less commonplace?'

I believe that everything becomes routine with time and as far as I am concerned, ordinary is not a bad thing. For me it represents normality, comfort, warmth and familiarity. Everyone has their own personal definition of ordinary. Some will go to great lengths to prove that they are indeed far from plain by dressing or behaving outrageously. Don't get me wrong, I'm all for individualism, as long as its not a false ploy to attract attention or to 'appear to be' extraordinary. I think it's crazy to believe that being ordinary makes you too normal and boring. What is normal anyway? Whose definition do we go by? I believe that being ordinary makes you real! Life is about typical people carving out an ordinary existence in the real world. We're all ordinary and whichever way we look at it, no matter who we are and what we do, to us, our lives often seem ordinary.

Several years ago I could only dream of being married to my soul mate, living in a wonderful home that we have created together, working from the comfort of my home and doing what I love best - writing. Indeed, many years ago this scenario would have been some extraordinary life I could only have envisaged and longed for. Today it is my reality. Today, it has become my ordinary life. You see, in the eyes of the beholder everything eventually becomes run-of-the-mill even if it once seemed an unbelievable dream. Even the most beautiful or handsome face becomes plain the longer you look upon it. Desirable possessions eventually lose their appeal and become tiresome the longer you have them.

The trick is to hold onto the magic by taking the time to really appreciate it all. There's nothing wrong with being an everyday person in an ordinary life as long as you regularly make the time to appreciate what you do have instead of taking it for granted or constantly wishing for what you don't have.

Multitudes of people have midlife crises because they suddenly wake up to the realization that they've become the boring and conventional family they once despised and looked down upon. In their mad and frenzied attempt to prove otherwise, they often ruin their perfectly normal life before realizing that it was in fact a happy one that perhaps just needed a little work. The wild excitement of an adventurous life soon proves to be short-lived and fizzles out, as extraordinary all too quickly becomes ordinary, for such is life!

Don't measure your life on whether it's predictable and uninteresting.

Measure your life on what you have - your loved ones, your health, your accomplishments, your home and surroundings and most importantly your happiness. At the end of the day the real question is 'Are you happy?' If ordinary makes me boring to others, then so be it. As long as I am happy with who I am and with my life, then who cares?

You see, it's all in the mind. I believe that every single one of us, no matter who we are and what our position in life, is ordinary. Sure, some of us do extraordinary things, but in reality we're still regular people, no one more exceptional than the other. Royalty may seem to have incredible lives to us, but even to them, their lives become tedious. Money may seem to buy an exciting life, but eventually it too becomes boring, habitual and even unfulfilling.

Sometimes we look upon another's life and wish we were living their life instead of our own, which seems so common and uneventful in comparison. But the truth is, that if you live in that person's shoes for long enough, trading lives so to speak, that life too will soon be accepted by you as usual and unremarkable. Perhaps you will then at last realize that you haven't got it all that bad. Remember what I said earlier about sitting back and thinking about what you do have and what's going right instead of focusing always on what you don't have and what's going wrong in your life and the world around you.

Why don't you do something extraordinary right now! Get a pen and paper and sit in a secluded spot. Now start writing down all the things in your life for which you have to be grateful. Doing this has a way of helping you to focus on the good in your life. Do this extraordinary thing (extraordinary because the usual thing to do is to focus on all the negatives) on a regular basis (once per week) and see how it adds value and meaning to your life. Do it now! Do it always!

So, to sum up and answer all my questions - yes, I see myself as an ordinary person living a pretty ordinary life; but I love my life - MY LOVELY ORDINARY LIFE! Learn to appreciate and love yours. If you're unhappy, then start doing something about it. Work at creating your own lovely ordinary life. You can start by appreciating the fact that you have a life!

How does this all fit into Dream Work? Well, before you start dreaming of what you don't have or what you want from life, you must first learn to appreciate what you do have. Then you can dare to dream about reaching for your goals and living your life to the fullest.

PARADISE LOST

Panoramic views stretch lazily as far as the eye can see.
Undisturbed Life, bursts with colour and vitality.
White, sandy beaches meet the waves as they spill sleepily from the ocean,
like Mother's milk for her innocent and peaceful Babe.
The birth of every new day is a celebration of Life.
Every moment in Paradise is an adventure of discovery and child like
fascination with endless possibilities ahead.
No sound, but that of Nature's song.
A place of harmony and calm.
A wondrous vision of breathtaking beauty and awe-inspiring innocence.
A Paradise lost!

PARADISE FOUND

Paradise is lost to so many people, for how can you find something if you
don't truly know what it is?
Is Paradise a place of extraordinary beauty?
Or is it a world of peace and harmony?
Perhaps Paradise is having all that money can buy, a situation of wealth,
power and unimaginable possibilities.
Or could it simply be a moment in Time,
when you have captured the essence of true happiness?
I believe our lives are made up of constant glimpses of Paradise.
These glimpses are moments in Time when we are blissfully happy and
overflowing with enthusiasm for Life and the overwhelming intimacy of
Love.
I keep all these moments close to my heart and look upon them often,
savouring each second of
Paradise found.

Sally Eichhorst

Chapter 13

Live Life To The Full!

If life is but a heartbeat,
may your drum beat strong and loud,
keeping a sure and steady rhythm
until you feel your music is played.

Sally Eichhorst

In order to live your life to the full, you must allow yourself the luxury of dreaming about your ideal life. Dare to dream and most importantly be prepared to take the risks necessary to make your dreams a reality. To explain exactly what I'm getting at, I'd like to share with you this thought inspiring story of a nurse and two of her late patients. This is her story...

"Henry and Albert were my patients and needed my full time attention. Bedridden and rapidly approaching the end of their long lives, they relied on me for care, company, treatment and understanding. I was their last contact with the outside world. It was while nursing them until their deaths that they taught me how to really live.

By the time I met Henry and Albert, they were both critical, high care patients who were expected to pass on very soon. They were both well into their eighties and slept most of their days away. I sat on a chair in between their beds and read while listening to their erratic breathing and occasional snoring. They were rarely awake at the same time and were never awake longer than an hour at a time. But when they were awake, they liked to chat to me about their lives.

Henry was a remarkable man who I grew to love and admire enormously. He recounted numerous stories of his long and well-lived life. Stories of great success, but nerve-racking risks. Stories of undying love and the special love of a father for his children and grandchildren. Stories of all the weird and wonderful places he had journeyed to and tales of his interesting experiences along the way.

I remember Henry would always wake up with a smile on his face and a wonderful memory on his mind. I often remember him repeating these words, 'What I remember most is full bellies, loud bellyaching laughter, great friendships, exciting places and unconditional love. What I remember above all, my dear is that I regret nothing. I had a love affair with Life and although my Life will end, the memories will never die.'

You see, Henry made the most of Life and Life in return made the most of him. He dared to live life to the full and was rewarded by a life rich in experiences, love, success and wondrous memories that outlast all else. Above all else, a Life with no regrets!

Albert, I also grew to love, but this was a sympathetic love, borne of pity. Albert's waking moments were a sad reflection of a wasted Life. He often awoke with a sad frown or would cry himself into consciousness and would weep all the more as he recalled a Life littered with wasted opportunities. The stories he told me were filled with regret for the risks he should have taken, feelings he should have expressed, the love and friendships he should have cherished and nurtured.

His life was laden with regrets and his mind was burdened with memories of what may have been. It saddened me that he still wanted to see and do so much to make up for the past, but had run out of time.

'If only young lady, if only…' he would repeat before dropping off again into a restless sleep haunted by a half-lived life of lost hopes, dreams and desires.

Albert passed away first. He was alone in death as in Life. Only I was there to comfort him and grieve his passing. His last words will echo forever in my mind until my dying day - **'I missed out on most that Life had to offer and now at the end, instead of memories all I have are**

regrets. Promise me that you won't do the same. Promise me that you'll tell as many people as you can, not to end up like me - full of regrets. Promise....' He said looking intently at me through weary bloodshot eyes. Only when I nodded did he close his eyes forever.

Henry passed away several months later and unlike Albert, his bed was surrounded by family and friends to grieve his passing, but also to celebrate the long, rich and fulfilled life he'd had. Henry went quietly and happily with a smile on his face while holding the hand of his oldest daughter. The room was filled with love, warmth and an abundance of wonderful memories.

After both Albert and Henry's passing, I came upon an interesting story written by Les Brown. It was as though the story was speaking about Albert. It spoke of a lonely, old dying man who wakes up to find that he is surrounded by a large group of people with loving, but saddened expressions. Unsure of who they are, but grateful for their support, he enquires whether they are his old childhood friends coming to say goodbye.

One of the people moves a step forward and gently takes the old man's hand. 'Yes, we are your best and oldest friends, but long ago you abandoned us. We are the unrealized hopes, dreams, and plans that you once felt deeply in your heart, but never pursued. We are the unique talents that you never refined, the special gifts you never discovered. Old friend, we have not come to comfort you, but to die with you.'

These powerful words by Les Brown were a chilling reminder of Albert's wasted life."

Life is something like a trumpet. If you don't put anything in, you won't get anything out. So if you find life is empty, why not try putting something into it.

W.C. Handy

"I was fortunate to come across Albert and Henry so early on in Life as they taught me how to really live. Since then I have come across plenty of people like Albert who are wasting their lives away, but only a few like Henry who really live Life to the full. I've made my choice - I've chosen to keep my promise to Albert by not ending up like him. I've chosen to be like Henry - to make the most of Life by living it to the full with no regrets, no 'if only's'. By recounting this story to you, I have kept my other half of the promise to Albert, spreading his message to as many people as I can.

So I encourage you to live Life to the full so that at the end of yours, you have wonderful memories instead of regrets. It's your choice!"

Do we try something new, or stick to the tried-and-true?
Do we ponder a thrilling adventure,
or contemplate what's on TV?
Do we walk over and meet that interesting stranger,
or do we play it safe?
Do we indulge our heart, or cater to our fear?
The bottom-line question:
Do we pursue what we want, or do we do what's comfortable?
For the most part, most people most often choose comfort the
familiar, the time-honoured, the well-worn but well-known. After a
lifetime of choosing between comfort
and risk, we are left with the life we currently have.
And it was all of our own choosing.
Peter McWilliams - "Do It! Let's Get Off Our Buts"

The best way to play dead is to risk nothing! Life is a risk and living it to the full is indeed risky business. Take some necessary risks in life - love completely, give freely, do willingly, speak openly and have your say while you still can, make a stand, realize your dreams and above all else, make your life worth living!

Life is a daring adventure, or nothing.
Helen Keller

BE ALL THAT YOU CAN BE!

In the beginning Life chooses you.
While you're an infant others choose for you.
As an adult, all choices are yours and yours alone.
If you want to lay blame or point fingers for the life you currently have,
you need not look far, for your finger should be pointed at yourself.
From the day you are able to make choices for yourself,
you choose how you will live.
At the end you chose the life you have led.

Sally Eichhorst

Chapter 14

Living The Life You Want Through Dream Work

Hold fast to your dreams, for if dreams die,
then life is like a broken winged bird that cannot fly.

Langston Hughes

D ream work is all about imagining what you truly want from our life. It sounds simple enough, but it's amazing how many people have no idea what they really want from life. Do you? Think about it. Do you have a plan for your life? In other words do you have any idea where you're going in life and what you want from life? To be exact, do you have goals?

If you have accomplished all that you have planned for yourself,
you have not planned enough.

Meddigo Message

To ensure success in life, you must work at setting goals. If you are not sure what it is you want to achieve to begin with, how can you possibly achieve anything? Imagine walking into a shop and not knowing what you want. You will probably walk out empty-handed or with something you don't really want or need. It's the same with goals. If you don't really know what you want, you will trundle through life aimlessly, never quite getting anywhere. Or perhaps you will achieve something you don't really want and live an unfulfilled life of wasted opportunities and potential. This is why it is vital that you have a clear and detailed idea of what your goals are.

The solution is to take the time to work on planning your life by setting clear and distinct goals. In other words, do some Dream Work. In fact this is the part that is fun, not work!

Really let your imagination run wild by allowing yourself to dream of what you really want from life. Forget about 'how', 'why' or 'but' and just keep those dreams flowing. At this stage we're not worried about anything else, other than what you truly want. If you keep thinking of how you will achieve it and why you can't, you are limiting yourself. Only when you cut out the 'how' and 'why' will your real goals in life become clear.

So don't limit yourself by not allowing yourself to imagine great and wonderful possibilities. Those who once achieved great things were just ordinary people like you and I, who had a dream and did something extraordinary by making that dream a reality. So can you.

Some men see things as they are and say "Why?" I dream things that never were and say "Why not?"
George Bernard Shaw

I now want you to get out a piece of paper (diary if possible) and a pen or pencil. Yes - now! Find a quiet spot where you can be alone for awhile and write down all the things you want from life. I mean all the things, whether it's something you want to do, a place you want to see, a person you want to meet, something you want to become or something you want to own. Even if you've done this exercise before sometime in the past, it is good to do it again as your goals and dreams may have changed with time and circumstances.

Remember not to limit yourself and rather to think big and exciting dreams for these are usually the ones you really want and you will also be more inspired to reach them. I repeat again, remember not to worry about how you are going to achieve them at this stage. Just decide what you want and write it down.

The most rewarding things you do in life are often the ones that look like they cannot be done.

Arnold Palmer

I encourage you to spend as much time as you can on this. Close your eyes and really dream. You can even spend a couple of days on really thinking about what you want from your life until your goals and dreams are clear to you.

To inspire you further, I urge you to read this list of goals and dreams as often as possible to remind you of the things you truly want from life. It will also keep you headed in the right direction.

It's a fact that to live the life of your dreams, you must have a distinct picture of exactly what you want from life. I encourage you to work on dreaming up some great possibilities. It's a start! Many have proved that their dreams and reality can become one. So can you!

It may be those who do most, dream most.

Stephen Leacock

Part 4

Ground Work

If only we planned our lives as well as we plan for major events,
for Life is indeed the biggest event of all!

Sally Eichhorst

Chapter 15

Plan Your Life

Many people have the right aims in life.
They just never get around to pulling the trigger.
Sunshine Magazine

♦ Ground work is a vital part of achieving anything in life. If you think about any project, whether it's a presentation or assignment that has to be put together or a house that is being built, the ground work has to be done first. Ground work is to your goal what the plans and foundations are to a house.

♦ This is the step where you ask yourself the question how am I going to achieve this goal? It involves a lot of research and planning depending on what your goal is.

♦ Unfortunately, this is often the stage at which most people give up on their dreams, as it just seems like too much hard work. As I said earlier, achieving your goals and dreams in life is often hard work, but well worth it if it's something you really want.

Opportunities are usually disguised as hard work,
so most people don't recognize them.
Ann Landers

♦   If you want to make your dreams a reality, you need to put in a
     little effort. Often it's not as hard as it seems and by just doing
     the necessary ground work and devising a plan of action, you
     are already well on your way to making it happen for yourself.

Chapter 16

Devising A Plan Of Action To Achieve Your Goals (Step 1- 5)

What is the difference between an obstacle and an opportunity?
Our attitude toward it. Every opportunity has a difficulty,
and every difficulty has an opportunity.

J. Sidlow Baxter

STEP 1.

Look at the list of goals and dreams you wrote down earlier. Now prioritize these goals from most important to least important. Let's start with your most important goal.

STEP 2.

If this goal is something you really want and desire, then what is stopping you from having it right now? You see, to achieve any goal, you must know what is standing in your way so that you can deal with the problem effectively.

I want you to answer the above question by writing down exactly what is standing in your way of achieving this goal. It is important to include all the possible setbacks so that you can plan and prepare yourself properly to avoid any nasty and unexpected surprises. Obviously, you cannot foresee everything that will happen, but good planning goes a long way towards preparing yourself effectively.

For example, if your goal was to be successfully self-employed, doing something you enjoy, some of your answers to the above question could be:

'I lack the finances to start up a business.'

'I can't leave my job as I need the money to live.'

'I have no idea how much it will cost and what I have to do to get started.'

'I don't know if I can do it.'

'I am not sure what sort of business to get involved in.'

'I don't know much about running my own business.'

STEP 3.

Now for each and every setback you wrote above, you must write down solutions to overcome them.

Believe it or not there is a solution to almost every problem you encounter, if you are willing to look at it from all angles and remain positive and focused.

If we again look at the example of becoming successfully self-employed, doing something you enjoy, some of the solutions to the setbacks mentioned could be:

'I could open up a savings or Investment account to build up some capital.'

'I could approach the Bank for a loan.'

'I could approach a Partner to share the financial risk with me.'

'I could start on a part-time basis from home before quitting my job.'

'I could study a part-time course on running your own small business.'

'I must do some research on various business opportunities by reading relevant magazines, newspapers and speaking to people.'

'I must think about what I really want to do and enjoy doing - remember the Dream section.'

'I must develop a belief in myself and work on thinking positively so that I will follow through with this goal. To keep motivated I will read motivational books and speak to other successfully self-employed people, to gain inspiration and ideas.'

Just look at all these solutions!

STEP 4.

Now that you have written down all the setbacks to achieving your goal and all the possible solutions to these setbacks, it is time to use this information to help you write down a clear, detailed and specific plan of action.

The easiest way to list your action steps is to look at your end result (what you want to achieve - your goal) and work your way backwards one step at a time until you arrive at something you can do right now!

This is where all the information in step 2 and 3 comes in handy. You can build some of the solutions in step 3 into your plan as well as adding other action steps along the way.

For example, staying with the same goal of becoming successfully self-employed, one of the last steps would be to employ staff. You would then work your way back until you found something you could do today. This could be contacting your bank to open up a savings or Investment account or to obtain a loan. You could also start by studying further part-time to learn more about running a small business.

These are all action steps, which you can start with and the great thing is that once you actually start you are already far more enthusiastic for that goal. Just making a start somewhere brings your goal a little bit closer and you start to feel that it's within your reach. But if you don't start, you will most certainly never finish!

STEP 5.

Next to each action step in your plan above, you must now write down a date of completion. This is very important as it stops you from procrastinating. It is a fact that when most people commit themselves to a deadline, they feel compelled to meet it and will go out of their way to do so.

Now your plan of action is complete
and it is up to you to move onto the next part.

Part 5

Dredge Work

The Beetle
There it lies on its back,
helplessly and desperately kicking its legs
in an attempt to land on its feet again.
Trapped and vulnerable,
its only hope a sympathetic human to give it a helping hand
or a strong breeze to lift and tilt it enough to right itself.
Until then, it's going nowhere!
It's stuck where it is
and no amount of struggling will help it to survive.
So many of us are like this Beetle!
We too are not moving, stagnant and misguided, we become trapped in jobs,
situations and relationships we are unhappy with.
We struggle to survive from day to day
relying on good fortune or opportunity to make itself known
and offer itself to right our circumstances.
However, good fortune and opportunity are masters of disguise and surprise.
An effort has to be made to recognize and act upon them.
Don't lie on your back,
kicking your legs in a tantrum, complaining about your situation and woes,
waiting for something to happen to make things better.
Do this
and you'll find as many Beetles do, that the true answer lies in never getting
yourself into that situation in the first place.
For if you must rely on other people or circumstances to make things better, you
may lie there, trapped and forgotten forever!
You must do something to change your situation. Take action!

Sally Eichhorst

Chapter 17

Time Is Fleeting

Life is short and finding time for the people and things you love may seem impossible. You must make the time!

Sally Eichhorst

You've just completed the planning stage and now this is the doing stage. Before I go on to explain about the importance of acting on your dreams, I'd like to remind you about the value of time. So often in life, we forget that time is limited and it doesn't come to a standstill while we sit around thinking about what we'd like to do with our lives. Yes, it's wonderful to dream, but be careful that your time doesn't run out before you start taking action to make your dreams a reality.

I've spoken to people and written on numerous occasions about the concept of limited time, but if the truth be known, it never really hit home to me until my Mom's time came to an end. I now understand at a deeper level the true meaning of this most precious and irreplaceable resource that we so often take for granted. I simply would not allow myself to believe that Time would run out for my mom and as is so often the case with most of us, I lived under the misconception that she and I still had all the Time in the world together. I believed I still had hours, days, weeks and years to talk to her and let her know how much she was loved. Like a fool I believed we could still do so much together and I could still help her achieve some of her dreams. I conveniently forgot the words I'd been telling others for so long - "Today is yours, but tomorrow is promised to no-one!"

Every night I fall asleep and my last thought is of her and every morning when I awake, my first thought is of her. If only we knew the exact time when someone we love was going to pass away. Then the last thing that person would hear would be words of love; the last thing they would see would be all their loved ones and most importantly the last thing they would feel would be warmth and love. I will never know for sure if Mom could hear us or sense our presence after she suddenly went into a coma. I can only hope and pray that she realized how deeply she was loved.

Sometimes it seems cruel for Time to end so abruptly for someone you love. I have come to understand more clearly that the only way to beat Time is to make the most of it. Never take it for granted. If there is one thing that is guaranteed in this world, it is that Time is limited - for you and for those you love. So cherish every moment in Time and **try** never to say "if only…"

I never expected to do exactly what I tell others not to do. But it seems that for a while at least, I am stuck with "if only's…" I can't seem to escape the thought that if only she had come to stay with me sooner or if only I had gone to stay with her sooner. If only I had forced her to eat more, to fight harder and somehow helped her more or done something differently that would have tipped the scales in her favour and made her better. Let me tell you "if only…" is a wicked thing, which I would never wish on anyone.

> *"Time is infinitely more precious than money,*
> *and there is nothing common between them. You cannot*
> *accumulate time; you can never tell how much*
> *time you have left in the Bank of Life.*
> *Time is life…"*

Israel Davidson

JUST A FEW MINUTES...

I was at the beach the other day lazily soaking up the sun and people-watching. I love to just lie there, listening to and watching all the colourful characters around me. I find people fascinating, especially when I can learn something from them. I learnt something that day...

A father and son dumped their belongings close by and proceeded to run at full speed into the ocean, leaping and whooping with joy. They swam together for a long time and then went to work building a large sandcastle. Father and son worked as a team, both as engrossed as the other, all the while chatting noisily and happily. Eventually the father tired and retreated to the comfort of his towel, stretching out lazily and fondly watching his son as he busied himself completing their large and well constructed sandcastle.

I had been watching them off and on for some time when the father called to his son "Come on Ben, we should be going now."

"Aw, Dad, just a few more minutes plea.....se?" pleaded the boy.

"Okay Son, just a few minutes," said the father smiling patiently at his son.

So the boy played on contentedly, building his fortress and imagining its occupants, chatting happily to himself.

A half an hour or more later the father again called out to his son "Okay Ben, it's time to go."

Again the boy pleaded, "Please Dad, a few more minutes?"

To my amazement, the father once more agreed to just a few more minutes and settled back comfortably on his towel to watch his boy at play.

Fifteen minutes later when the father once more told his son it was time to leave, I was sure he would become impatient and angry when the youngster again pleaded for just a few more minutes. Surprisingly, he relented once more saying "Alright Ben, just a few more minutes and then we'll mosey on home."

In my opinion 'just a few minutes' were up a long, long time ago. This man seemed to have all the patience and time in the world.

He suddenly became aware of being watched and before I could guiltily avert my gaze, he said "You probably think I'm a real pushover giving in to him all the time? Well, his mom and sister were killed in a car accident six months ago and I would give anything to spend just a few more minutes with them. I was always too busy and never had enough time to watch Amy playing. My wife, Sue always said I should make more time for her and the kids. It took just a few minutes for my life to change when they died. So much can happen in just a few minutes. Now if my son asks for just a few minutes of my time, he can have it. To tell you the truth, I get to watch him playing for just a few more minutes and the pleasures all mine."

I was speechless and gulped hard with a lump in my throat.

The man called his son again and this time the boy obediently came running, a happy grin on his face and sand all over his little body. Father and son walked off hand in hand and I was left pondering the meaning of life.

It's true, that just a few minutes can change your life and that of those around you. Just a few minutes can add up and become your life. This is why we should make the most of every minute available to us. Who knows when our minutes or those of someone we love may run out? Take just a few minutes to think about this.

Make a point of not using time or words
carelessly as neither can be retrieved.

Sally Eichhorst

THINK!

Think twice about complaining about Life
as so many are facing Death.
Think twice about choosing to give up
as so many are never given a choice.
Think often about what you do have
and little about what you don't have.
Think often about the good in your life
and let go of the bad.
Think of every struggle as a victory
and an opportunity to learn and grow.
Think of every second still available to you
and know that you can make a difference.
Think about it!

Sally Eichhorst

Chapter 18

Learn To Hang Up Your Problems And Worries

Hang up your problems before they hang you!

Sally Eichhorst

nother important area to touch on in this section - the "doing" section of dredge work, is being able to handle problems along the way. If there is one thing that is guaranteed in life it is that you will come across all sorts of problems, whether personal, physical or career orientated. These problems will hamper your progress towards living the life of your dreams if you are not able to deal with them effectively.

A friend told me about an interesting character who had worked with her. Apparently this guy was one of the country's top advertising executives. This man was forced to deal with loads of stress on a daily basis. Every day had its share of problems ranging from manageable to explosive. His day was made up of crisis meetings, brainstorming sessions, trouble-shooting and roller coaster deadlines. Nail-biting decisions had to be made, one after the other and nothing ever seemed to run according to plan. There were always problems! This guy "rail-roaded" his way through everything, like a steam train on maximum throttle and at the end of every hair- raising day, he had a peculiar ritual.

On his windowsill in his office, he had a lovely little Bonsai tree.

Every day before leaving work to join his wife and children at home, he would spend at least fifteen minutes fiddling with the tree, pruning, snipping, touching and talking earnestly to it. Only after this daily ritual, would he leave the office for the comforts of his home.

My friend and numerous others had witnessed this strange habit of their co-worker on many occasions and were clueless as to the meaning of it all, if indeed there was any reasoning behind it.

One day my friend found herself working late into the evening to beat a deadline and her tree pruning co-worker kindly offered to give her a lift home. En route to her home, he stopped off at his house to tell his wife what had happened. His wife insisted that my friend join them for dinner.

My friend noticed that while her co-worker was with his family, he was a changed man. The tension and stress so evident at work were gone. He was totally calm and relaxed, as though he had not a care in the world. The conversation around the dinner table revolved mainly around the children and consisted mostly of light-hearted stories about what had happened during their day. His wife added a few amusing comments about her exploits and they spoke of future holiday plans and weekend getaways. He said nothing about his day and his overwhelming mountain of problems, some of which he'd dealt with and others, which still loomed ahead.

My friend was amazed at this man's restraint. If she had had a day like his, she would be desperate to vent her anger and frustration and share her problems and worries. Yet, here he was, as placid as a lamb, listening attentively to his family's small talk, when all the while his mind must have been jam-packed with ideas, decisions, choices and consequences far more important than his family could possibly have imagined.

Afterwards, as he was driving her home, her curiosity got the better of her. "How do you do it?" she asked. "How do you undergo such a remarkable transformation from stress-riddled high powered executive to placid, well-balanced family man?"

"It's my little 'problem tree'," he chuckled. He explained to her that he had met a wise old Japanese man many years ago when he was still learning the ropes and trying to make a name for himself in advertising. The old man was the head of a large international corporation and my friend's co-worker was a junior executive on the team handling the corporation's account. Surprisingly, the old Japanese man liked the fresh and radical ideas of the youngster and as a gift for a job well done he gave him a little Bonsai tree. The old man told him that it was a 'problem tree'. He said that he himself owned a number of these trees and he was adamant that it was partly due to these little trees that he had managed to build up his small empire and still live a happy and balanced life. The old man showed him how to care for the tree and explained to him the secret of the 'problem tree'. "And I've never looked back," said my friend's co-worker with a smile.

"So what's the secret of the 'problem tree'?" asked my friend inquisitively.

"Well, every day before I leave the office for home, I first take care of the tree as the old man showed me. I prune and trim it ever so slightly and carefully, all the while talking to it about the problems I encountered during the day. You see, it is said that the 'problem tree' actually feeds off these problems. I touch the branches of the tree very lightly, hanging all my problems up for the day so that I don't have to take them home with me. The tree likes having the problems as companionship for the night and I like leaving them behind so it's a mutually beneficial relationship. It suits me because my problems don't belong at home with my wife and children and it benefits the tree because it gives it something to think about over the long and lonely night ahead.

The funny thing is that when I get back to my office in the morning to reclaim my problems from the tree, many of them are gone, others seem smaller and more manageable and for the rest, the answers just seem to come to me. Crazy, huh? But it sure works for me!"

You shall not take problems to bed with you, for they make very poor bedfellows.

Unknown

I agree! Problems often need to be put aside and hung out to dry for the night. In the morning they've either blown away or after a restful night you are able to see them more clearly and tackle them more effectively.

Don't ever let your problems be an excuse.

Anon.

Why don't you try and hang up your problems for the night. Sometimes if you give yourself time to relax and stop fretting and worrying all the time, things look a lot better. Some people get themselves so worked up and stressed that if they don't start hanging up their problems, they're going to literally hang themselves. Control your stress or it will control you!

No matter how hopeless the present problem may seem, remember the age old saying: *This, too, shall pass.*

STOP AND THINK

Sometimes it's time to just stop and think.
Just put everything aside and rest assured, your ship won't sink.
Some of us fly through Life on turbo engines, hardly stopping to refuel before we head on to the next joint.
Frantically we rush from here to there, so often missing the point.
We never stop long enough to admire the scenery or give Life a chance to show us the beauty, opportunity and potential it offers to everyone at a glance.
So take time out now and then to stop and think about what you have, what you've done and what adventures may lie around the bend.
Think often about Life and what you want from it and remember most of all to enjoy every bit of it!

Sally Eichhorst

Chapter 19

Dealing With Stress Before It Deals With You!

I try to take one day at a time,
but sometimes several days attack me at once.

Jennifer Unlimited

With today's hectic pace while we're trying to carve a life out for ourselves, we must also learn to manage our time properly.

Are you juggling too many roles to perfection, taking on too much work, always in a frenzy to meet deadlines, so busy that your head's spinning and you have absolutely no time for yourself? Well, if this describes you then I've got news for you - you're totally stressed-out and you'll soon be ready to crack if you don't remedy the situation.

The strange thing is that many people feel that they have to always be overly busy in order to have value in society. These days the common reply to 'How are you?' seems to have become, 'I'm so busy' or 'I'm totally stressed-out'. The words 'busy' and 'stress' seem to have become associated with successful, high-powered business people or energetic, productive people who don't waste time and are respected.

Sure, it's good to keep your mind busy and fill your time with productive activities, but it's not so good when overly busy becomes a norm and "stressed out" describes your every waking hour. Granted, a certain amount of adrenaline is necessary to get you up, moving and active. However, too much adrenaline and activity leads to a stressed out, frustrated, agitated and resentful individual, who is constantly filling his or her head with endless lists of things to do and places to be as well as constantly reminding him or herself just how difficult life is.

There seems to be a serious misconception in society today, that the more stress you are under and can handle, the more you are respected as a "go-getter" on the road to success.

Anyone can teach themselves to handle as much stress as they like. You can teach yourself to tolerate more and more stress because it is a known fact that your present level of stress is exactly equal to your tolerance to stress. It sounds like a mouthful, I know, but basically it means, increase your level of stress a few notches and your tolerance to stress will naturally increase too. So what's the problem? Well, adopting the approach of trying to teach people to handle more stress will result in them taking on more and more stress until they either have a physical or mental breakdown. The physical breakdown could be in the form of a heart attack, stroke or an alcohol or drug addiction to help them cope. Alternatively, they could suffer a mental breakdown in the form of chronic depression or a complete nervous breakdown to show they're definitely not coping.

The solution is simple. Don't try to teach yourself to handle more stress. Instead work on teaching yourself how to keep your life as stress free as possible. I've watched people literally age overnight due to too much stress. I've seen friends have nervous breakdowns before the age of 20 and others with all sorts of physical ailments - ulcers, hernias, high blood pressure, heart problems to name but a few - all as a result of stress. Countless others have estranged loved ones due to bad tempered outbursts and a loss of emotional control as a result of 'stress overload'. So no one can tell me that stress is good and being able to tolerate loads of it makes you a power-house, go-getter and a mountain of strength. Because there will come a time when some cracks will appear and that mountain of strength will erupt into a deadly and uncontrollable volcano of destruction.

I remember mentioning to a friend that I play squash to help me relieve occasional stress. She replied that she didn't believe it was humanly possible to only have occasional stress and it was unrealistic of me to make such a statement. Sadly, I have to disagree. I have created a life that is as stress free as possible, not because I feel I can't handle stress, but because I don't want stress. It is unhealthy physically and mentally and I do my utmost to keep my life free from it. Instead of increasing my tolerance to stress, I have lowered my tolerance to stress. I literally refuse to become stressed out! I have also found an outlet for the occasional stress I do have - exercise! Squash, running, gym - it does the trick for me!

I challenge you now to try and keep your life as stress free as possible. Try it - just refuse to become stressed out. The results will astound you! Not only will you be physically healthier, more relaxed and clear-headed, but believe it or not, you'll also be more effective, efficient and a great deal happier.

Life is fragile, so handle it with care!
Sally Eichhorst

**Come on, it's time for a change a fresh start!
Let's see how to make your life less stressful.**

1.   Firstly, you need to make a firm decision to take charge of your life. If you're stressed out, you need to realize that your lifestyle at present is dangerously unhealthy and it will come crashing down around you unless you accept that changes need to be made and then make a firm decision to make them.

2.   Making a firm decision commits you and drives you to take the action required to make changes for the better. So many people are unhappy and frustrated with their lives, telling themselves continually that they really must do something about their situation, but they never seem to get around to it. They never seem to find the time in their set routines to make changes for the better.

You simply have to make the time to take action and make some positive changes.

3.   The aim of all these positive changes you make, must be for you to do all you can to create a tranquil, stress-free and harmonious home and work environment for yourself. How?
This could include: -

- Becoming better at delegating when required. This includes work and home life. Share the load more at home with your partner and give chores to children. At work, you also need to realize that you can only do one thing at a time. If there's too much to handle, delegate!

- Take on a hobby to help you relax.

- Learn to say "No!" Trying to please everyone, all the time, is almost always impossible and eventually it will take its toll in the form of a mental or physical breakdown or moody, snappy behavior. No one will love you any less or respect you any less if you occasionally say "No" to preserve your own sanity. Be more self-assertive about your limits and stop taking on too much.

- Work on your own self-management in order to plan your day correctly. In other words your diary should not be jam-packed with one thing after the other, leaving no room for flexibility, unforeseeable mishaps, travel time and simply some 'time out'.

- As much as you insist that you do not have any time for yourself, it is crucial that you make some personal time available on a regular basis. You just have to make it happen! Go for a long walk or run. Do some gardening. Have a massage. Read a book in the garden. Just do it!

- You must also realize that you can only do one thing at a time and as long as you do so to the best of your ability, no one can possibly complain.

-   It helps to also distinguish between important and urgent. More often than not everything is urgent, so rather concentrate on the important things first and then do the rest. (learn to prioritise)

4. You need to adopt a new attitude and approach to your life. You must realize that your own wellbeing is just as vital as hose you love and work with. You literally need to spring clean your life and stop trying to be perfect. Adopt a new interest in your own wellbeing and work on boosting your self-esteem. It is a fact that people who feel confident and have a sense of self-worth, feel justified to also give themselves some quality time and attention without feeling guilty or self-involved. I challenge you to let go of the old and start anew with a clear head, more time for yourself, greater flexibility in your life, more fun and far less stress.

5. Often people add to their stress by negative talk. What I'm talking about is those of you who come home from work and all you discuss is the numerous bad things that happened that day or you heard about that day. This is very draining for someone listening and it also makes you re-experience those bad things. The only thing this succeeds in doing is to make you even more uptight. Rather stick to the positive aspects of your day. Who needs the extra stress of reliving stressful moments?

6. Overall you need to strive for a balanced life. A balanced life is a happy and stable one. If something is not balanced, it usually falls over. In the same respect, if your life is not balanced, you may find it falling apart around you. Concentrating too much on any one area of your life leads to neglect in others. You really must work at getting the balance right. You need to start enjoying every day of your life, instead of rushing through them and wondering how you coped the previous day and how you will be able to handle tomorrow.

For many people who are stressed-out, it is self-created problems that can be dealt with if they make some changes as discussed above. Make these changes and aim for a stress-free way of life!

Judge your success by the degree that you're enjoying peace, health and love.

Unknown

MY GARDEN

I have been living here for some time now, yet I saw the garden for the first time today. Every day it's there, exposed and splendid in its beauty. I wonder how I ever went by without noticing each bold, crispy, green blade of grass, each individually shaped intricate leaf and the strong, proud and confident trees reaching for the skies.

Suddenly, I'm drinking in all the colours and seeing it all as if for the first time. I feel like a puppy, with each new discovery a joyous adventure.

Standing there in the early, crisp morning light, I took a long, deep breath of Life. I took a long, hard look at my garden, not only seeing, but also appreciating, enjoying and absorbing its stark beauty.

I should do this more often, in fact, I should do this every day for it awakens me to the beauty around me, the depth to all things.

All things are deeper than their outward appearance. Take the time to really look and appreciate the beauty and goodness around you. Take time out from your hurried and stressed existence to see and feel the wonders of the world around you. Enjoy it all while you still can!

It is a sad truth that many, if not most of us, rush through our lives, the older we get, the more time seems to fly and the less time we seem to have to really see and appreciate the people and the things around us. It's so important to stop every now and then, take a step back and look at life. Look at the people in it, the things in it. Do you really know and appreciate what you have? Do you ever stop to really think about it and take it all in? Try it sometime, it's quite refreshing and somehow relaxing!

Sally Eichhorst

Chapter 20

Achieving Your Dreams Through Dredge Work

I can give you a six-word formula for success:
"Think things through then follow through."
Edward Rickenbacker

I t's now time to go back to your plan of action in part 3 and start with action step one, physically doing it and then moving onto the next step. As you complete each action step, tick it off and move on to the next one until all action steps have been completed and you have accomplished your goal.

This is where many more people abandon their dreams, as there just seems to be too much to do before they reach them. They feel overwhelmed by the enormity of it all because this big dream they have seems so far away and so unattainable at present.

Ideas not coupled with action, never become bigger
than the brain cells they occupied.
Arnold H. Glasow

This is why it is so important to do something every day, no matter how small, to move you closer to your goals. Even your biggest goals will eventually be broken down into smaller, more achievable ones if you keep chipping away at them on a daily basis. Everything is manageable if you break it down into smaller parts and deal with each small step one at a time. Before you know it you will have accomplished this once out of reach goal.

DREDGE WORK INVOLVES DOING AND PERSEVERING!

> *The trouble with many of us is that in trying*
> *times we stop trying.*
>
> **Unknown**

Doing the hard labour of dredge work is great, but it is no good if you give up when faced with the first obstacle. To succeed it is vital for you to learn to persevere. When something goes wrong with your plan and you fail to achieve what you wanted, you must try again. Too many people give up too soon and often they were so close to succeeding if only they had tried once more.

> *Triumph is just an "ump" ahead of "try."*
>
> **Anon.**

To truly enjoy the rewards of achieving your goal, you must be prepared to dredge on regardless, rising again after every fall to try once more.

> *Energy and perseverance can fit a man for*
> *almost any kind of position.*
>
> **Theodore F. Merseles**

With a little effort, you too can develop perseverance. Anyone can develop this quality by following the few easy guidelines below:

1.`   Work on developing strong willpower. Some people persevere and succeed by sheer will. If you put your mind to it, you can achieve almost anything.

2. Learn from your failures and use what you have learnt to make you stronger and wiser for your next attempt. I don't really like to use the word mistake or failure. Instead of saying that I made a mistake, I like to say that I learned a valuable lesson. When scientists are in the process of experimentation, the "failed experiments" are vital to the process and it is these so-called "failed experiments" that often lead to the experiments that eventually "work". Oscar Wilde hit the nail on the head when he said "Experience is the name everyone gives to their mistakes."

> *More people would learn from their mistakes*
> *if they were not so busy denying them.*
> **J. Harold Smith**

3. You must make some progress every day towards the attainment of your goal - no matter how small.

4. Realize that a lack of perseverance is a bad habit, which you can stop by practicing again and again the art of persistence. In other words, learn to finish what you start. This is a major failing in most people. They never seem to be able to follow through with anything and see it through till the end. Practice finishing projects, like an incomplete painting, fixing your car which you started ages ago, finishing extensions which were supposed to be completed months ago, completing a course you started and lost interest in. The object is to practice perseverance in your every day life and it will eventually become a habit to persist until you achieve everything you set out to do.

> *We are judged by what we finish, not by what we start.*
> **Anon.**

5. Learn not to fear obstacles, but instead to see them as challenges that you can learn from and may even hold hidden opportunities.

6.   Always think of the rewards you stand to gain by achieving your goals. If the rewards are great enough you will be all the more driven and motivated to persevere until you reach the end goal.

7.   Keep your mind focused on the big picture, which is the achievement of your goal and not on short-term fixes. This means persevering until you reach your goal rather than allowing yourself to be tempted by short-term benefits or instant gratification. Learn to hold out for 100% later rather than opting for only 2% now. This means some sacrifices, but surely you would rather sacrifice 2% now, rather than lose 100% later.

An obstacle is something you see when you
take your eyes off the goal.

Anon.

Once the backbreaking dredge work is over, it's time to do some maintenance work.

Part 4

Maintenance Work

Maintenance is all about keeping up a certain standard.
Whether it means adjusting or changing for the better
or just keeping up the good work,
the aim is to maintain your momentum forward
toward your goals and dreams in life.

Sally Eichhorst

Chapter 21

Maintenance Work

*The secret of genius is to carry the spirit of the child into old age,
which means never losing your enthusiasm
and never being afraid to try something new.*

Aldous Huxley

A n important part of achieving your goals and creating the life
you want rests on your ability to constantly change and adapt
where necessary. This is what maintenance work is all about.
It's not just about maintaining your progress one step at a time towards
your goals, but also about being flexible enough to change when and
where you must. Being able to change quickly and effectively keeps you
one step ahead of obstacles and competition. It also keeps you on your
toes and allows you to learn and grow.

Most people are afraid of change. They resist it because it makes
them feel uncomfortable and insecure. It is those people who are open to
change and who are constantly looking for better and easier ways of
doing things that are far more likely to succeed in life. They are always
improving themselves and their situations, diversifying, expanding and
trying out new technologies and procedures.

If you have to, you must be able to change direction. Try adopting a
new attitude to obstacles; change the way you think about certain things.
The point is, you must not be rigid in your thinking and stop fearing any
change of plan. Change is not the enemy. Without change there would be

no growth and progress in the world. Learn not to fear change, but rather to fear your inability to deal with change - that's the enemy!

Work on steadily maintaining your progress towards your goals and adjusting when necessary and soon they will be yours. Keep it up!

Chapter 22

Be Willing To Change

"Change is often a message to move in a new direction; to start afresh!"
Sally Eichhorst

Restructuring, reengineering, reorganization - call it what you want, it's rife today in most industries and countless companies. The result in most cases is FEAR. The fear of downsizing or retrenchments, short time, no increases or bonuses, a step back on the ladder of authority, a forced relocation - in a nutshell 'change'.

Change for most is often troubling. It causes anxiety as comfort zones are shaken and uncertainty sets in. It's human nature to enjoy a certain degree of security and continuity. A place to come home to, a semi-flexible or structured routine to follow, a place to go to work with the promise of a salary every month indefinitely. Change unsettles this security and is therefore unwelcome.

Today, companies have to be able to change in order to survive. They have to be flexible and adaptable to keep a competitive edge. Restructuring is often a case of 'do or die' and changes are inevitable.

Just as companies have to be flexible and adaptable enough to change, so do people. It's the people who can adjust and make the best of a situation and who can even spot hidden opportunities in a potentially negative situation, that survive best.

It's really all a matter of perception. Too many people perceive change as negative. Before they've even looked at the situation from all angles, they perceive it as a threat to their security.

Babies and toddlers are faced with more changes in a day than most adults would face in a year. They embrace these changes, which become challenges and opportunities to learn. Without change there is no growth. Think about it - if a man has been with the same company for 30 years doing exactly the same thing, with no change whatsoever in his job description - does he have 30 years experience or 1 year, 30 times repeated? I firmly believe that he only has 1 year, 30 times repeated. To gain experience there must be change - extra responsibilities, extra studies, courses, learning another aspect of the job.

Every year you should be able to add something new to your C.V. to show that you've grown. Just the smallest change denotes at least some growth. It could be personal, physical or career orientated, as long as the end result is constantly bettering yourself and your situation. This means changing for the better!

> *Change means growth. Growth is the only evidence of life. So*
> *when you've stopped changing, you stop living.*
> **Sally Eichhorst**

Learn not to fear change. See it as a challenge. If it's negative, use it as a learning curve to help you grow and remember to constantly look for hidden opportunities.

I remember speaking at a breakfast meeting for an organization catering to 'Women In Business'. The room was filled with successful businesswomen from a variety of industries across the board. I was most impressed with the lovely lady sitting next to me, not because she presented herself in a beautiful and impeccably mannered way, but because of her amazing success story.

After chatting to her for some time, I could see why she had progressed so well. She was literally bubbling over with enthusiasm and ideas. Her energy and vitality were quite unique and I found myself fascinated by her story.

She had worked for the same Computer Company for many years. Although she was in a dead-end job, she enjoyed working with computers and it was nice to have the security of a steady income. But then she was retrenched along with a number of co-workers and her whole world seemed to come crashing down around her. She took the retrenchment personally as so many do and went into a deep depression. She felt like a failure, as though it was a personal reflection of herself and her work, an insult to her pride. She feared for her future and was overwhelmed by feelings of insecurity and worthlessness.

Her depression lasted for several weeks and it was with a great effort that she eventually pulled herself together and started to see things more clearly and in a different light. She decided that it was time to start trying to see the brighter side of her situation, namely, she had been paid a substantial retrenchment package, she had years of invaluable experience, she was still young enough to start afresh with another company.

Indeed, when she began to look at things from a different perspective, she started to see more and more positives and possible opportunities. She began to research the idea of opening up her own computer training company using the expertise she had gained over the years and the money from her retrenchment. Suddenly, she had direction again, a will to live and grow and she had rediscovered her pride and self-worth again.

A few years later, she had 4 successful computer training branches throughout the country. I looked at this accomplished, self-made and successful lady and was delighted as always to hear about the triumph that so often comes after darkness and difficult change.

You see, often in our darkest hours, we are forced to change and that turning point, if seen in the correct light, can often hide life-enriching and life-changing opportunities, if only we choose to see them and make use of them.

Opportunities are hidden from those who are blinded by negativity.
Sally Eichhorst

I'm sure you have read about the days when diamonds were first discovered in South Africa. Many wrote about the multitude of people who flocked to South Africa from far and wide in the hope of striking it lucky. They often worked themselves into the ground for months on end with nothing to show for their effort but a broken spirit and wasted resources. Many lamented their rotten luck, questioning the unfairness of it all.

It is said that countless poor men had in fact struck it lucky, but had failed to recognize the opportunity before throwing it away.

How is this possible? Well, in the beginning these men sold up all their belongings to invest in basic supplies and they enthusiastically put their heart and soul into working their claim. They started out optimistic and hopeful, sifting carefully through stones, ever watchful for that special stone, the diamond. Days of backbreaking hard work would stretch into weeks, weeks into months and sometimes, even years. Then, on one of these long hot days, one of them would be impatiently sorting through the stones like a robot, when he would come across a diamond.

However, because he was so used to not finding any diamonds and automatically throwing each stone back into the river, he would inadvertently throw the diamond away before he even realized what he had done. You see, he had formed such a strong habit of throwing each stone back into the depths of the river, that when the one he was actually looking for appeared, he still threw it away. And so it was with many of these Fortune Hunters, who had actually found what they were looking for, but had failed to recognize it and then threw it away.

In life it is so easy to fail to recognize an opportunity, even when it has landed in the palm of your hand. Failing to recognize these opportunities, we so often and so easily throw them away and then bemoan our fate.

Stay awake and alert, for opportunities are everywhere, some more hidden than others are and some even staring you in the face right now. Often we only see these opportunities when we are forced to change. Change forces you to see things through different eyes and therefore see things you would otherwise have overlooked.

Chapter 23

Change
Even If It Means Turning Your Life Upside Down

You're always alone, but you're only lonely
if you don't like the person you're alone with.
Wayne Dyer "Staying on the Path"

C hanging your life for the better isn't easy. In fact, doing the right thing often means doing what may be more difficult or uncomfortable. Indeed, to create the lives we want, we often have to turn our lives upside down and start all over again.

This reminds me of an interesting, ancient Hawaiian legend. According to this legend, every person born to this earth brings with them a bowl of pure and bright light. This is known as their life-light.

If the person takes care of their life-light, the light will shine ever more brightly and will radiate strength, which will flow through the person, showering them with special gifts of blooming health, tremendous strength and all-knowing wisdom.

But if the person is not careful, their light may be obliterated by a dark shadow. Every time the person hurts another in anger, has a tantrum for not getting their own way, shows signs of jealousy, hate, envy or any other negative characteristic or action, a stone falls into their bowl of light.

Just one stone in the bowl will cause the light to fade a little. A few more stones will cause more of the light to go out. If stones continue to fall into the bowl unchecked, the light will eventually go out altogether and only darkness will remain.

The person now has a bowl full of stones - a heavy load to carry. The stones will weigh the person down until they are forced to stand still, unable to move, eventually becoming stone themselves. A stone can never grow or move and most importantly, it cannot live.

There is only one way to change this unhappy situation and allow the person to escape life as a piece of rock. The person must decide for themselves to turn their bowl upside down, thereby throwing out all the stones they have collected and starting all over again with an empty bowl full of life-light. You see, it's never too late to start again and learn from previous mistakes. However, no one can tell the person or force them to start again. It has to come from the person. It takes great effort to start all over again, but the reward is well worth it.

Of all human resources, the most precious is the desire to improve especially because the largest room in the world is the room for improvement.

Anon.

It's never easy to decide upon change and to start again. Whether it's bettering yourself, your situation, your relationships or your health - deciding to change for the better takes effort and determination. Yes, it often does mean turning your life upside down, but often if you don't, you'll be just like the person whose bowl is full of stones - stuck in an unhappy situation, unable to move or grow and ultimately unable to live life to the full. Only you can decide to make changes and again I repeat - it's never too late!

To the question of your life, you are the only answer.
To the problems of your life, you are the only solution.

Jo Coudert

JUST START!

"Where do you start?
The best place to start is wherever you are today."
Arthur Caliandro Simple Steps

People often ask me the same thing when pondering a problem, planning a goal or trying to change something. "Where do I start?" Problems and goals often seem so big and overwhelming that people are scared off before they even begin. The same goes for making changes. Often it just seems like far too great an effort and people would rather settle for second best because it's more comfortable and less risky.

My first bit of advice, as simple as it may sound, is always the same - just start! It's so important to just get started. Often taking action and getting started gets the ball rolling so to speak and before you know it, you're well on your way to solving your problem, reaching your goal and making some positive changes in your life.

Stop looking for excuses, stop looking for an easy way out and stop lounging around thinking about things - start taking some action and get moving.

The next thing I tell people, follows the age old saying, "As long as you're moving in the right direction, it does not matter the size of your steps." So the trick is to first get moving and then to keep taking steps in the right direction, even if they're baby steps.

It's often best to start small. Break down a big problem into many small ones and keep going at them one at a time. Eventually, before you know it, you will have solved what you once thought to be a colossal and impossible nut to crack.

A mountain climber doesn't physically get to the top of a mountain by only thinking about it and he certainly does not get there by doing it in one large leap.

He starts at the bottom and slowly makes his way to the top, step by step. Every step in the right direction, no matter how small, brings him closer towards his goal.

In the same respect, if you want to make some major changes in your life, then start now. It need not be a mind-blowing and earth-shattering move, but just something small to indicate a start and to encourage you to go on.

There are always going to be many obstacles that will stall our momentum in our journey of life. When we come across these stumbling blocks, we can either sit around doing nothing, worrying about how we are ever going to overcome them, or we can simply make a start. How? By doing the very best we can with every single day available to us. Try and do something small every day to move you closer towards your goals, to solve that major problem you have or to make positive changes in your life.

I'm sure many of you have heard the story about the man who tried to change the world. For those of you who haven't, I'll tell you his story.

As a young man, he started out trying to change the world. When he realized that it wasn't working, he then tried to change his country. Again he realized that this too wasn't working and he then attempted to change his hometown. It took him some time to realize that he couldn't change his town and so he eventually tried to change his family.

By this stage he was already an old man and it only dawned on him at this late point in his life, that the only thing he could truly change, was himself. He then realized that this is how he should have started many years ago as a young man. He should have started small, working first on changing himself. Through changing himself he could have made an impression on his family and they in turn could have made an impact on his hometown. This impact could have influenced a change in the country and ultimately this could have changed the world.

Consider how hard it is to change yourself and you will understand what little chance you have of trying to change others.

Jacob Braude

That's why, if you want to change the world, you should start by changing yourself! Start small, but do start!

To change yourself, look at what you fear and what you hate. Start there.

Wayne Dyer "Staying on the Path"

Chapter 24

Work On Building A Life And Not Wasting One

Some people get the breaks; some people make their own.
Some people succeed because they are destined to,
but most men because they are determined to.

Anon.

The late Irving Stone spent many years studying great people such as, Freud, Darwin and Michaelangelo. He said that all achievers had a common characteristic in that they had a vision or dream of something that they wanted to accomplish. They would then take action, going at it and keeping at it even after years of getting nowhere, often being knocked down again and again. The difference between these people and many others is that they always got up and at the end of their time, even if they had not accomplished their dream or vision in full, they had achieved a great deal of what they originally planned to do.

'Most people spend their lives constantly reacting to events and experiences, rather than taking action to create the lives that they want. They float about in a distracted, hap-hazard fashion, without direction and clueless, in the end achieving very little and looking back with shock at the situation and life they alone have created. The men who try to do something and fail are infinitely better than those who try to do nothing and succeed.'

Lloyd James

Build your life carefully, with attention to detail and never be willing to put up less than the best. You are like a carpenter who has been given the wonderful, once in a lifetime opportunity, of building his dream house. Surely he would build wisely, planning and acting on his ideas, using quality materials and employing all his skills to create a worthwhile masterpiece. You should do the same with your life. Build a life worth living so that you may look back on it with pride and joy, not regret and pain.

> *Never say you failed,*
> *but rather that you tried!*
>
> **Sally Eichhorst**

This brings us to the end of the 6-part Work theory. Let's recap:

Part 1.   Mind Work

Part 2.   Character Work

Part 3.   Dream Work

Part 4.   Ground Work

Part 5.   Dredge Work

Part 6.   Maintenance Work

The next chapter is for all those people who feel that their journey through life has been a tough one. I hope that you will realize that there is always someone far worse off than you who would trade places with you in a flash.

This chapter is also for those few who know the true meaning of hardship and suffering and have still managed to make the best of their situation, never giving up. These are the people I truly admire.

Chapter 25

This Illness Wants A Fight.
I'm Giving It A War!

Don't give up when you still have something to give.
Nothing is really over until the moment you stop trying.

Nancye Sims

I'd seen him on many occasions at the gym and had stopped for a quick greeting every now and again, but I'd never really had a proper conversation with the good-looking, young, blonde man before. I now waited impatiently at the gym's cafeteria not really knowing what to expect from our first conversation.

At last he arrived, a lovely, wide-mouthed grin on his handsome 27-year old face. His lively eyes, sparkling with intelligence and mirth spotted me and I watched as Darryn Smith approached with ease and confidence. It occurred to me as I waited that I'd hardly ever seen him without a friendly and approachable smile on his face.

At 7 years of age, Darryn's parents first noticed that he had a slight co-ordination problem. Even a simple task like carrying a glass of water proved difficult without spilling half its contents. At the time it wasn't very noticeable and his concerned parents thought he might grow out of it.

At 11 years of age, his little co-ordination problem had progressed, causing him difficulty in walking. At the same time his baby sister, Simone, then only 3 was diagnosed with Leukemia (cancer of the blood).

While Simone underwent chemotherapy, Darryn was evaluated by a group of neurologists and the diagnosis was a rare genetic disorder with no known cure or treatment - Friedreich's Ataxia (FA).

"I knew after reading the relevant literature that one day I would be confined to a wheelchair, but being as young as I was and still being able to do what any ordinary kid does, it made it hard for me to believe." recalled Darryn.

At this stage Darryn's problem wasn't an issue. It was simply a small walking problem overshadowed by his six month stay at Johannesburg General Hospital watching his little sister fight for her life.

"She endured so much pain and the chemotherapy made her so ill and thin. She threw up more times than I could imagine. That little girl went through so much. Seeing what she went through and her determination to fight made me so much stronger."

Simone died just after she'd turned 6, a week before Darryn's 13th birthday.

"Seeing what a beautiful, innocent child went through has made my family mentally incredibly strong and if I hadn't been witness to the pain and suffering that Simone went through, I don't think I would have been able to handle my illness in the way I do."

At 16 years old Darryn's disorder had become very noticeable, particularly after spending 2 weeks in bed with the flu. When he was strong enough to get out of bed, he realized how quickly his condition had progressed. He had lost a lot of the feeling around his mouth making speech difficult and his walking ability could be compared to that of a drunkard. It was a frightening discovery, which Doctors blamed on his inactivity while he had had the flu. Friedreich's Ataxia is a slow progressive disorder, which influences the cerebellum of the brain affecting motor actions such as walking, talking and any other skill involving movement and co-ordination. Inactivity worsens the condition causing motor skills to rapidly deteriorate. A neurologist compared it to a car, which is left in the garage too long. Eventually its battery goes flat. Sadly, unlike the car whose battery can be recharged, the damage done to Darryn's motor skills is presently irreversible and the only advice doctors could give was for him to keep active in an attempt to strengthen and maintain his motor skills.

Darryn was determined not to give up. His Dad bought a home gym and Darryn went to work on his body every day, willing it to grow stronger.

Back at school everyone noticed that his walking and other physical abilities had dramatically changed. His illness was now more obvious and being a teenager he became very self-conscious and emotional especially when he was teased and mocked by the older boys. It was difficult to keep his chin up and pretend that he wasn't hurting. He then made a courageous decision to leave and attend a special school for the physically disabled. In 1989 he attended the Open Air School. "I'd never seen anything like it. It was so hard for me to see what I saw. At first I felt I didn't belong there. It was hard to face and I was frightened by the prospect of getting worse. I cried my heart out after my first day. Surely I didn't belong there?"

Darryn's strength and character triumphed and eventually he came to accept his new surroundings. "This school showed me the true meaning of determination, perseverance and dedication. My disability, compared to most of them, was not a disability but rather an illness, which they would rather have had. This made me appreciative of the ability I still had."

In his early twenties, his walking had become really bad. With stubborn determination in the early months of 1996 he joined a corporate gym, The Health & Racquet Club. He remembers the first day he walked awkwardly into the gym using a crutch for balance while his left arm was used for co-ordinating the movement of his legs. In late 1996 at the age of 22 he rolled into the gym in a wheelchair.

"I am and remain always an optimist. From the moment I was forced into a wheelchair I was determined to get out of it. I used to believe that one day I would walk, I now know I will! I am not about to let some illness destroy my life!

I don't want people to feel sorry for me. Rather I want people to let me be an example of what you can lose. All I want is for people to really understand and appreciate what they have. People must realize what they have now! It's too late when it's gone. I know what it's like to walk and run. Now its been taken away from me and more than anything in the world, I want it back.

People just don't take the time to think about what they have. Sometimes you've just got to tell yourself everyday how lucky you are to have your health, the ability to walk, talk, run, see, hear and live a normal life. I've been there. I've lost so much, but I'm determined to get it back. If I could only make people understand and see things as I do now.

My problem is that I'm trapped in this body. I feel like no one really knows Darryn. I know that when I can walk and run again, I will always appreciate it because of what I've been through. I will always know what it means to go without and not to have the things that most people take for granted.

For me life is a challenge. I love to be challenged and believe me there is nothing more challenging than my condition. It's made me a very strong person and I am all the more determined to fight and triumph over this illness.

It's no good for me to be depressed over my situation. I've got to make the best of it and I'll give what ever it takes to beat it. At a very low point in my life, when I was younger, I was inspired by a poem called 'Follow your Dream' and that's what I'm doing. My dream is to retrieve what I once had. I believe I will walk. I want to tell people that they can be and do anything. If I can be so motivated, positive and happy, then why can't they?"

FOLLOW YOUR DREAM

Follow your dream
Take one step at a time
And never settle for less
Fast continue to climb
Follow your dream
If you stumble, don't stop
And lose sight of your dream
Press onto the top
For only on top
Can we see the whole view
Can we see what we've done
And what we can do
May we then have the vision
To seek something new
Press on and follow your dream.

Unknown

Looking at Darryn, I don't understand how people can get upset about silly little things. There are so many people who are depressed for no apparent reason. They're just disillusioned with life. Then I look at Darryn whose making the most of his situation. He wants to get better and absolutely refuses to give up. He has a wonderful sense of humour and carries a huge smile with him everywhere he goes. Even in his situation, he's living on the bright side of life, seeing hope and good in everything and everyone. If only we could all learn from this young man and let him be a shining example of what life is all about - not giving up!

Through the internet, Darryn has made contact with a number of people in the U.K and the U.S.A who suffer from Friedreich's Ataxia (FA) and various other forms of Ataxia. One was a 53 year old man in the U.K.(Dave) who was only diagnosed 5 years ago with Cerbal Ataxia(CA). In America a man, now 58 years old was only diagnosed 2 years ago with FA. Doctors say you are born with the condition and it can strike at any time, affecting some more than others.

Darryn joined a network of people with FA in America to keep up to date with new developments in its treatment. Various experiments are being conducted and in the last 3 - 6 months a lot of progress has been made.

"My objective is to seek medical help in one of the first world countries in an effort to eradicate this illness once and for all. With the increasing advancement in medical break through I feel a cure is inevitable."

The problem is that this condition is so rare. Not many people suffer from it (approx. 2000 people in U.K., only 3 known in S.A. and approx. 150 000 in America with various types of Ataxia) Therefore it is relatively unknown and untalked about resulting in not enough time and money being injected into research. Darryn truly believes that they are close to finding a cure if only there was a greater awareness so that more energy and resources are put into the research.

" The fact is that Ataxia isn't a priority but I'm willing to make it one. I have lived 27 years with this illness and enough is enough, it's time to make my dream a reality. I used to believe that they will find a cure. Now I know they will. I keep myself mentally and physically strong at the gym so that when they test anything on me, my body will accept it and will triumph over this illness. I will try anything and do anything to overcome this."

Darryn is currently preparing for a trip to the U.K. to meet with Dave, the 53-year old man mentioned earlier. 2 years ago this man was in a wheelchair and much like Darryn, he too was determined to get out of it. Hearing about how oxygen helps people with cerebal palsy, which has similarities to various forms of Ataxia, this man decided he had nothing to lose by trying an experiment. Every day for 3 months, he went into a decompression oxygen chamber.

No one could believe it when after 3 months, he discarded his wheelchair and could walk again. "The effects of Oxygen Treatment (HBO) may have a different affect on my form of Ataxia, but I will never know until I try. If it can help him, it can help me. I'm prepared to go that far. Why not?" said Darryn challengingly.

"I am and remain an optimist, an achiever, a fighter. I'm going to walk for Simone, my family and for everyone that knows me. This illness has deprived me of so much, the ability to drive, to do so many things without having to rely on others, to walk, to run, my independence, but although it has taken so much away from me, it has definitely made me a better person. It has developed my patience, my determination, my perseverance and my attitude. I will never give up. This illness wants a fight; I'm giving it a war!"

Darryn Smith is indeed an inspiration to me and to everyone he knows. I live in hope that by the time you read these words, Darryn will be walking again.

> *Life is like riding a bicycle.*
> *You don't fall off unless you stop pedaling.*
>
> **Anon.**

The final chapter of this book is dedicated to Dale Rene' Berman. If the world had just a few more people like you Mom, all would be well. Until we meet again...

Chapter 26

A Fighter To The End

HOPE

Afraid of what lies ahead, she faces this mighty adversary.
The battle is a fierce and drawn out struggle of mind and body,
but she is victorious.
Life's victory is short-lived as the enemy returns.
Why conquer at all when the battle seems so endless?
Why not just give up?
It would be so much easier.
No!
Never give up for it is in the conquering that we grow
and eventually become larger and stronger than the monsters,
which plague us.
Hope is the key! Where there is Life, there is hope.
Hope is the driving spirit, which fuels our desires.
It gives us the will to go on when we think we cannot.
Where there is hope, there is a way.
Never give up Hope and most importantly:

NEVER GIVE UP!

Sally Eichhorst

In Life there is but one secret to success, which influences not only who you are and what you have achieved, but can also mean the difference between life and death. What is this secret to success, which is so important that even your very survival depends upon it?

NEVER GIVE UP!

I am honoured to know a very special person. Someone I have come to know as the bravest and most determinedly strong individual I have had the pleasure of sharing my life with thus far. It's a strange thing how those who are the bravest and strongest among us are often the last to acknowledge their strength and bravery. If only she saw the courage I see, the utter determination to fight on in spite of the endless battle, the agony, the illness and the fear. Somehow she is always ready to do battle again, fighting with every ounce of will and strength to survive.

I sat at her side in the hospital, holding her hand while she slept fitfully. Looking down on her pale and drawn face, I remembered the two of us laughing together just the other day. All our good times came tumbling into focus - memory upon memory of mother and daughter, together forever. I felt so helpless and frustrated sitting there. I wanted to see her laughing, to make her happy and comfortable, to lessen her pain and make her body strong and healthy again. So I'm selfish - I want my Mom forever!

Mom's been fighting cancer for almost fifteen years now. It's been a long and hard struggle and she has persevered throughout. Chemotherapy, although the treatment, is almost as ugly a monster as the cancer itself and its effects are often devastating. Mom's gone through it all countless times and her body is weak, battered and tired, yet her mind is strong. Without her even realizing it, in fact she would even deny it - she's an unbelievable fighter. I take my hat off to her and all those who will not give up. I am awed by the strength it takes to fight against something so powerful again and again. I don't know if I could do it. It takes a special kind of person - quietly brave, with an inner-strength more powerful than even she is aware of, to fight constantly against the dying of the light.

TO MOM

There's a very special person who loves me like no one else can.
This person felt me deep inside and knew me intimately
before anyone else did.
She watched over me,
believed in me and supported me through all the ups and downs.
No one could ever replace this special person in my life.
I love you mom!
Thank you for fighting against the dying of the light,
because I still need you.
I know it's selfish,
but I want you forever and I'll fight this thing with you forever!
You are my light, my beacon of strength and I'll be lost without
you.

LOVE ALWAYS, SALLY

Mom, like so many others fighting this devastating monster called cancer, has taught me that there is but one secret to success in everything you do:

NEVER GIVE UP!
I love her all the more for proving these words to be true. She's never given up on life and still fights on.

I wrote the words you've just read a few days before Mom was due to visit me on a two-week holiday. About three weeks before I had written this, I had been up in Johannesburg for business and ended up canceling the majority of my appointments, as Mom became severely ill in reaction to her chemotherapy and was hospitalized. I spent hours and days holding her hand and willing her to get better. She recovered sufficiently to return home and I truly believed she was getting stronger.

Although Mom was still weak, we all felt that a two-week holiday with me at home in Durban would do her good. She arrived here so weak and pale, leaning heavily on a walking stick and dressed like an Eskimo in a blizzard. From the moment she arrived, she went almost immediately to bed and there she remained unless I tried to force her to bath or to get a little fresh air in the garden. She refused to eat and I found myself in a constant state of panic, feeling guilty for trying to force feed her like a naughty child, yet wanting so badly for her to eat to build up her strength.

She seemed to deteriorate by the hour and I grew more and more desperate. Never did I imagine the severity of her condition. I constantly looked for excuses why she seemed to have given up. I thought that perhaps she was depressed because her oncology specialist had told her that they were forced to stop her chemotherapy midway, as her body could no longer handle its poisonous strength. I believed that her spirit had been broken and it was my duty to build it up again. I never once believed that it was in fact a shutting down process. Her body was slowly shutting down and she was withdrawing more and more with each hour. I know now that on a deep, subconscious level, Mom knew that she was dying. She had come to me to say good-bye. Within only 4 days of her arrival I was forced to say good-bye to her forever.

Mom passed away at exactly 12.45 a.m. on Friday, 28th July 2000. I know because I was there holding her hand, no longer helping her fight to the end, but rather loving her and being with her until the end. She held out a lot longer than any of the Sisters at the hospice believed she would. This was because she was a fighter. Mom always underestimated her own strength when in fact she was one of the strongest and bravest people I knew.

For everyone who has ever watched someone they love die, I now understand the pain and devastation that you endured. Up until then, I had never even seen a dead body before. This experience has changed me forever. The loss is indescribable, the pain excruciating, because there is nothing to dull it. Without this special person, my life will never be the same again. A part of me is lost forever and there is nothing anyone can say or do to make it better. They say that time heals all wounds, but secretly I know that this wound will leave a deep scar that will never be forgotten. Sure, life will go on, which somehow seems unreal when someone you love dies, but life will never be the same.

To die at the age of 50, with so much of her music still unsung, is a shame. To have lived for so many years, in a constant fight for survival and often in pain, is a sin! All I ask of everyone reading this, is that you make the most of your life to make up for all those who couldn't. If you have life and health, then you have more than many were ever given. You have a chance to live life to the full and make every moment count. I also encourage you to really appreciate your loved one's, never taking them for granted. Don't wait to show them how much they're loved and never put off saying or doing anything you could do and say now. Believe it or not, tomorrow may be too late. We only realize what we had when it's no longer there. This is not just a cliché; it's the truth!

What I have come to realize today, is that Mom never really did give up. She simply quietly accepted and prepared for her death. I know it seems an odd thing to say, so I'll try to explain. Sometimes when you're faced with a possible fight or flight scenario, you have to look at all your options and take action. When all options have been exhausted, sometimes the brave thing to do is not always to fight on regardless, but rather to make peace with the enemy and to accept defeat graciously. It's a matter of knowing when to back down. I know now that this is what Mom did. She fought this ugly cancer for over 15 years and exhausted all her options. She knew when to back down and now I must learn, as must all those who loved her, to let go.

> *"Even from the other side, you're watched over fondly my child.*
> *Go well, live a long, fruitful, happy life!*
> *I love and cherish you always,*
> *Mom"*

Extract from a letter Mom wrote to me weeks before her death, with the instructions that it should only be given to me upon her death.
Dale Rene' Berman - 17. 8. 1949 - 28.7.2000

MY LIFELINE

One never quite realizes the fragility of life, until faced with death.
In a matter of seconds, a life can be snatched away.
No arguments, no comebacks,
no chance to undo what's been said and done.
It is impossible to say good-bye to someone you love.
No matter how prepared you think you may be,
there is nothing to dull the pain of loss, when it finally arrives.
For once I find myself at a loss for words.
Death has silenced me.
The pain is indescribable, as I fight a torrent of feelings.
My heart sinks like a storm bruised ship,
every time I think too deeply and remember too clearly
what I no longer have.
Fighting to keep my head above water,
free from the depression so keen to suck me under and drown me
with despair.
My only life line, the support and love of the living.
Those who we so often take for granted, our family and friends -
our loved one's.
These are our lifelines!
Look after them and always work on strengthening the bonds,
which may one day save your drowning soul.

Sally Eichhorst

LIVE

L LEARN

I INSPIRE

V VALUE

E ENTHUSE

LEARN   From the moment we are born, we are learning. Life is a learning experience! The aim is to put to good use what we have learnt along the way and to constantly learn more. No one ever knows it all. Indeed the beauty of life is that there is always so much more to learn.

INSPIRE Inspiration is a wonderful and powerful tool that can drive people to greatness. To be able to inspire another is to lift them to greater heights, filling them with the positive energy and enthusiasm needed to make changes for the better. Inspiration is food for the soul and one can never be satiated. Throughout our lives, we should aim to inspire others and to constantly spark the flames of our own inspiration to succeed and be all that we can be.

VALUE   One of Life's most important lessons is value. Value for ones self, for all those around you and for all things. Sadly, many people lose value for themselves along the way, believing that they deserve the scraps that Life offers them. Everyone and everything has value. Above all else, you have value. Value and respect yourself and others are sure to value and respect you more. Life is so fragile and therefore has immense value, just ask someone who is terminally ill and still wants to do so much more with their life. Also learn value for those around you. Family and friends you so often take for granted are irreplaceable, their value immeasurable. Sadly we often don't realize the true value of another until they are gone. Learn to value and respect all things living and inanimate and you will have earned the right to be valued and respected yourself.

ENTHUSE Enthusiasm is the spice of life. It makes life so much more interesting and fun. Enthusiasm is also seriously contagious and others will soon be infected with yours. Approach all things with enthusiasm and you will captivate imaginations and nations!

The Journey Ends...

Life is not just one big problem to be solved. Rather, it is a mystery to be experienced, all the more meaningful and beautiful when it is shared and celebrated with other persons who are committed to "growing deep, not just tall!"
Karen Kaiser Clark, The Centre For Executive Planning

I have discovered that if there is one secret to life, it is to live it to the fullest with no regrets and 'if only's'. The only way to uncover the true mystery of Life is to experience it completely. Life itself is a beautiful and exciting puzzle, with each new found piece, a discovery of growth.

My parting advice to you is that it is never too late to really live. It's up to you to give life your all and build a life worth living.

I challenge you to be all that you can be, by working on the six parts covered in this book. Look back over what you have read and ask yourself if you are doing everything possible to build a life free of regrets and full of meaning and achievement.

Is your life an adventurous journey or a constant uphill battle? If you still see your life as a constant uphill battle, you need to read this book again and again and again (yes, I meant to repeat it three times) until you realize that life is what you make of it, no matter what the circumstances.

I can honestly say that my life is an adventurous journey as I am living the life of my dreams; a life which I have created. Anyone can do it. If I can, you can!

Although our journey together has come to an end, yours has only just begun...

I am convinced that life is 10% what happens to me and 90% how I react to it. And so it is with you. We are in charge of our lives and attitudes.

Rev. Charles Swindoll

MY WISH FOR YOU

May your journey through life be an adventure
of discovery and growth.
May everyone you meet warm your heart and soul both.
May you live long and well
And may laughter fill your every cell!
Above all else,
May your life's song be long and sweet!

With love from Sally

These then are my last words to you:
Be not afraid of life.
Believe that life is worth living,
and your belief will help create the fact.

William James

More Titles from the same Authors

Unleash Your Full Potential
Warren Veenman & Sally Eichhorst

This popular bestseller has been reprinted several times and is in constant demand. Its popularity stems partly from being so easy to read and to understand. It is filled with simple and practical programs, principles and philosophies, which are easy to follow and show you how to achieve and live your dreams.

The purpose of this book is to help you unleash your full potential and create the life of your dreams, whether this means more money, fame, power, love, or happiness. By the time you finish this book, you will have the knowledge and skill to succeed, irrespective of your age, physical status, background, financial situation, or education.

People from all walks of life insist that reading this book was one of the best decisions they ever made. It helped them succeed beyond their wildest expectations, just as it can help you.

Where Has My Ceiling Gone?
Warren Veenman & Sally Eichhorst

- If you have ever dreamed of bettering your life but never thought it possible, this is the book for you!
- We invite you to read this book and embark on an amazing journey that can improve every aspect of your life.
- This book is built around a fable that reveals how one man discovered the secrets to success. Let them become your route to success.
- Discover the nine life skills, which can lead you to achieving all your dreams in life.

Dare To Succeed

Warren Veenman & Sally Eichhorst

This thoroughly entertaining and thought inspiring book acts as a reminder that there is absolutely nothing stopping you from succeeding in life, but yourself.

The main aim of this book is to show you how you can succeed by working on the following five important areas.

- Awaken the Power Within (Positive thinking)
- Attitude and Understanding determines success
- Conquer the "Big 3" (Fear, Worry, Depression)
- Make the most of your Time
- Dare to reach your Dreams (Goals)

We assure you, when you reach the last pages, you will have all the tools necessary to succeed in life.

Get Your Act Together

Sally Eichhorst

This attention-grabbing book simply demands a reaction from the reader. The book contains 11 harsh but bold statements meant to kick-start you into getting your act together. The stark and brutal truth will shock some readers and rightly so, as the aim is to rattle the reader's cage into taking some positive action.

A Pocket Full Of Inspiration
Warren Veenman & Sally Eichhorst

This delightfully entertaining and talked-about little book is a power pack of inspiration and gives new meaning to the phrase "Dynamite comes in small packages."

The book is filled with amazing and thought inspiring true-life stories, which are sure to have an impact on you. The overall aim of this little gem is to lift your spirits and motivate you to greater heights. It is sure to be a moving and heart-warming reading experience, which will definitely be worth your while.

This is an excellent gift for anyone, whether for you, that special someone in your life, friends, family, clients or staff.

A Little Burst of Inspiration
Warren Veenman & Sally Eichhorst

This little gift book is an ideal keepsake filled with wonderfully entertaining and inspiring stories to warm the heart and exercise the mind. It simply bursts with inspiration!

All these books are available at your local bookshop, or can be ordered direct from the publisher.

...inspire the world
with words.

Reach Publishers

Self-publishers and Distributors of all books

www.aimtoinspire.com